"Like the Stars of the Heavens"

by
Helen Zegerman Schwimmer

JAY STREET PUBLISHERS, NEW YORK, NY 10023

Library of Congress Cataloging-in-Publication Data
Helen Zegerman Schwimmer

ISBN # 1-889534-38-2

Published by Jay Street Publishers, New York, NY 10023

For My Parents
My Husband and Our Children
And Their Children

Contents

"Like the Stars of the Heavens"

(Genesis 22:17)

Introduction

It was a few days before Chanukah. I was driving home from the local mall, my trunk overflowing with games and toys for my three children, when the car suddenly slowed to a crawl. I nervously steered it to onto the grassy shoulder of the highway and hit the emergency brake. The gas gauge registered empty.

This was back in the days before cell phones, so there was nothing to do but pop open the hood and wait, hoping a Good Samaritan or the highway police would eventually stop. But when the cars continued to whiz by, I grew increasingly impatient and decided to hike to the nearest gas station that I had passed about a quarter of a mile back on the Belt Parkway.

"My car ran out of gas on the highway," I sheepishly confessed to the gas station attendant.

"Can't spare anybody right now," he said. Instead, he offered to fill a two gallon can halfway and I trudged back down the road, like the biblical Rebecca hauling her jug from the well. It wasn't until I removed the cap from the can that I realized the spout was missing, so I had no way of pouring the gasoline into the tank.

As the sun started to sink, so did my spirits. Why me? Why today? Why here on this busy highway that was beginning to feel like a desolate stretch of desert? The answer would arrive shortly.

I watched the battered car pull off the road. It was a red Chevy, just like the model my father used to drive. While a child peered out at me from the rear window, a young woman emerged from the driver's seat. She walked purposefully over to the trunk, opened it and removed an object, then turned and came towards me, smiling broadly.

As she handed me the tin can with the spout, she said with an unmistakable Hispanic accent, "I bring this for you. . .you need this!"

And that's how it's been for most of my life. Inexplicably, a stranger will mysteriously appear to provide me with exactly what I need at that moment, whether it's a life-saving boat, a partner for life, a life-altering Shabbos meal or a can with a spout.

Hashgacha Protis, divine providence, has brought extraordinary people into my life, like E. Edward Herman. The E. stands for Eliezer (G-d was my help) and that says it all. Like our patriarch Abraham's right hand man, this Eliezer, who is well into his eighties, is a visionary whose wisdom, limitless energy and generosity of spirit continues to be a source of inspiration for those of us who have been blessed with his friendship. As a young G.I. he influenced my life with his heroic deeds on behalf of the St. Ottilien Displaced Persons Camp in Germany where I was born, and then he reappeared a half-century later to become my most enthusiastic fan. Not content just to read my articles, he encouraged me to "write a book." This volume is the direct result of his gentle persuasion.

The title comes from the promise G-d made to Abraham to make his offspring "like the stars of the heavens." (Genesis 22:17) But unlike the fleeting stardom of celebrities who walk the red carpet, the essence of the stars who shine in this volume – including rabbis, doctors, educators, lawyers, entrepreneurs and writers – is their inner light which guides them to lead lives of purpose and meaning, illuminating the way for all of us.

Originally published in **The Jewish Press** between 1994 and 2005, the articles collected in this anthology reveal a parallel universe where Jews don't *kvetch*, they *kvell*, about their meaningful relationships, their good fortune and their faith. Each section is introduced with a personal vignette, which often reveals the back story behind many of the stories. And epilogues have been added to several of the original articles to provide you with "rest of the story."

As a *baalat teshuvah*, (a returnee to my roots and religious observance) I have experienced the broad spectrum of Jewish life with friends and relatives who define themselves as Modern Orthodox, Conservative, Reform, black hat, convert or unaffiliated. So whether I'm writing about a Yale student battling against enforced coed habitation, or a follower of *The Grateful Dead* who becomes a follower of the Lubavitcher Rebbe, their stories also reflect my own complex journey along our diverse contemporary Jewish thoroughfare.

When my family immigrated to America in the early 1950s, the buzzword was assimilation and the strategy was to quickly integrate foreigners into mainstream society by housing us among the general population. Very often I was the only child in a class of thirty whose family had "come over on the boat." When my mother spoke Yiddish to me in public, I would cringe, embarrassed that our refugee status was exposed to anyone within earshot.

Although there were no ESL classes, I was a voracious reader and ultimately excelled in my second language, earning my B.A. degree in English from Brooklyn College. When I had children of my own, I took great pleasure in sharing with them the linguistic joys of the language with books like *The Cat in the Hat*.

A mere generation later, who could have predicted that the language of the *shtetel* would become so trendy that this childhood classic is now available in Yiddish? I have even met "Yiddish Speakers," people from all over the country who descend on New York where they can practice and polish this newly rediscovered tongue. Once earmarked for extinction, Yiddish, like the people who spoke it, is not only alive and well, but thriving on theater stages, across the pages of best-sellers, and in the streets of the most cosmopolitan city in the world. And now I even find myself explaining to my own non-Yiddish speaking children why I neglected such a meaningful part of their heritage.

As you read these stories, which have been revised and edited for publication in this volume, you will find the non-English words italicized. A glossary is provided at the back of the book to define these unfamiliar words which, unlike *schlep* and *kvetch*, have not yet become an integral part of the American lexicon. Some words are Hebrew in origin, while others may be Polish or Ukrainian and still others German, reflecting the journeys of our ancestors over the millennia, like the stars of the heavens.

Helen Zegerman Schwimmer
April 2007

I

I Look Taller
in The Jewish Press

*J*erry Greenwald, the general manager and managing editor
of **The Jewish Press** newspaper, towers over most of the staff at the
publication's Brooklyn headquarters, but since I write from my home
office we rarely had the opportunity to stand side by side. When Jerry
and I finally did meet, he peered down at me and remarked with good-
natured puzzlement, "Somehow I thought you were taller."

"I look taller in **The Jewish Press**," I shot back, straightening
my 4'9½" frame. I wasn't alluding to the photograph which
accompanied my byline, but to the lofty company I keep. My columns
about the extraordinary achievements of giants in the fields of medicine,
the arts, politics, religion, education and the media appears to have
dramatically enhanced my own modest stature.

The seminal article that introduced me to the quarter of a million
readers of the world's largest Anglo-Jewish weekly was **A Taste of
Shabbos**, remembered by many because it included a fool proof recipe
for parve rugelach. The week the article was published I was shopping
in the 47th Street Photo Store in Manhattan. A salesman, whose
children are my husband's patients, told me that when he praised his
wife for her tasty rugelach, she pointed to my article. The next day,

when he asked for more of the delicious pastry, they were all gone, all six dozen.

After reading my article, Irene Klass, the publisher of **The Jewish Press,** *whose generosity of spirit is legend, called to tell me how much she enjoyed my writing. And so began a warm working relationship with this indefatigable woman who, with her husband, Rabbi Sholom Klass z"l, were pioneers in the world of Jewish journalism. The newspaper they so carefully nurtured from a modest local publication has become recognized internationally as an influential and powerful unifying force for Jews around the world.*

During their lifetime Rabbi and Mrs. Klass met and entertained mayors, governors, presidents and a queen, almost. Shortly after her coronation, Britain's Queen Elizabeth visited New York and invited Mrs. Klass and other prominent Jewish leaders to tea. But when her daughter became ill with a high fever, Irene Klass was reluctant to leave her sick child and announced, "The Queen will have to do without me."

Another revealing story concerns the time Rabbi Klass was invited to meet with President Reagan. Mrs. Klass had written a complimentary profile of the first lady that she wanted to share with her, so she enlisted Rabbi Klass's help. But when he entered the White House, he was asked by an aide to surrender the newspaper. However, upon greeting the President Rabbi Klass pulled out a spare copy of **The Jewish Press** *from his coat and proudly told Mr. Reagan, "My wife, Irene, wanted you to see this."*

Irene Klass and I have seen eye to eye on many things, and not just because we're both the same height. As the editor of the Woman's Page, located strategically in the newspaper's centerfold, she literally had her finger on the pulse of the Jewish community, so I never knew where a phone call from Irene would lead me.

A groundbreaking international women's conference or breaking news about the controversy involving Orthodox students at Yale University were all part of her domain. When we needed a picture to add punch to the Yale story, a friend lent me her son's sweatshirt which bore the university's motto, "Light and Truth" in Latin and Hebrew. No one ever suspected that it was Irene, always the good sport, who modeled the shirt for the crucial photograph.

*The day my investigative article on the **Yale 5** was published she proudly informed me that William F. Buckley had written about this controversy in his syndicated newspaper column that day, and even articulated several of my own ideas. Since our weekly paper had gone to press a couple of days earlier, Irene Klass was thrilled that we had obviously scooped him.*

The Yale 5: Divinity vs. Diversity

When Yale University opened its ivy gates to welcome women in 1969, who would have guessed that *co-education* would eventually become a synonym for *co-habitation.* Rabbi Daniel Greer certainly didn't. Dean of the Yeshiva of New Haven, Connecticut, Rabbi Greer is the father of a Yale freshman who was threatened with disciplinary action.

And just what was his daughter's "crime?" Because of her religious convictions, Batsheva Greer chose to live off campus in defiance of Yale's new dorm regulations. Along with Lisa Friedman, Rachel Wohlgelernter, Elisha Hack and Jeremy Hershman, this group of Orthodox Jewish students who challenged the housing rules at Yale University became known as the Yale 5.

"Up until two years ago," Rabbi Greer explained, "if you were a resident of the New Haven area you were exempt from living on the Yale campus and were permitted to live at home."

Rabbi Greer's older children who attended Yale did just that. Now Yale has rescinded that policy and extended the dormitory requirement to sophomore year as well. This new ruling affects Batsheva Greer as well as freshman Elisha Hack, who is also a New Haven resident. When these students requested exemptions on religious grounds, they were unilaterally denied by Betsy Trachtenberg, Dean of Student Affairs.

"When I attended Princeton 40 years ago," Rabbi Greer recalled, "four male students were expelled when females were found in their dormitory rooms."

Who could have predicted that the pendulum would swing so far? Now all twelve residential college dormitories at Yale are co-ed. Each dormitory has a heterogeneous mix of 400 students that are representative of the entire student population and each is a microcosm of the university which is evenly split in terms of males and females. Approximately one third of Yale's five thousand students are Jewish and forty to sixty of these are Orthodox.

Permission Requested

"We spent a year and a half dialoguing with the university, face to face, phone calls, letters, faxes and they refused to budge," said Elisha Hack.

The students have hired prominent Washington attorney Nathan Lewin, and "unless Yale waives its residence requirement, we may have no choice but to sue the university to protect our religious way of life. We are asking only that Yale give us the same permission to live off campus that it gives any lower classman who is married or anyone twenty-one years of age," said Elisha. He urges the school to "come up with a reasonable appeals process to remedy the situation." For instance, married students must show a certificate and if you're over 21 you have to present a birth certificate.

"I'm sure there is a way to demonstrate proof of religious conviction," he added.

Sophomore Jeremy Hershman of Long Island offered to do just that by providing the dean with letters from his rabbis documenting the religious basis for his request for alternative living arrangements. In his letter to Dean Trachtenberg, dated March 18, 1996, Jeremy wrote that it would be impossible for him "to adhere to his religious restrictions and obligations while living in university dormitories." He went on to assure the dean that he would make "a personal commitment to participate fully in campus functions" to honor the policy of integrating freshmen into the diversity of campus life.

Dean Trachtenberg's reply, dated April 15, 1996, emphasized that although she plans to continue the practice of working with students to accommodate their religious practice, she must deny his request because "the housing rules are based on our very strong belief that living in a residential college is at the very center of a Yale education."

Moral Support

Tom Conroy, the Deputy Director of Public Affairs and spokesman for the university, said Yale does not plan to create other exemptions. "There is always going to be a conflict between people's individual beliefs and the society in which they live. The university is not obligated to compromise its principle of the value of living on campus."

When it was pointed out that Yale accommodates students' religious beliefs regarding their dietary laws, so why not basic housing requirements, his response was "you have to draw the line somewhere. Every school has requirements that are attractive to some students and may disqualify it for others."

Rabbi Greer argues that "Yale's attempt to impose its new morality on any religious person is offensive. It's even more offensive," he continued, "that when a person objects, Yale's attitude is 'go to the back of the bus.' This is mean-spirited and narrow-minded."

He goes on to ask, "Why should an Orthodox Jew not avail him or herself of the best possible education? Are they saying we can't get a top education unless we abandon our principles? What's going on in Yale's dormitories shows a violation of anyone's principles as well as anyone's religion."

As an example of this, freshman Rachel Wohlgelernter cited a conversation she had with a Muslim classmate in the Hillel dining hall. The kosher facility attracts many non-Jewish students because it serves "the best food on campus." According to Rachel, this student confided that the co-ed living conditions made her equally uncomfortable. Rachel attended Yeshiva University High School in Los Angeles and then deferred coming to Yale while she spent a year studying at Michala in Jerusalem. Noting that her modern Orthodox family firmly supports her position, Rachel said that she was taught at an early age to stand up for what she believes in.

"I'm not out to exclude or segregate myself," Rachel

stressed. "I am amenable to a single-sex dorm or a single room. However, rooms are chosen by lottery, so if you have the luck of the draw you might get a room that has its own bathroom."

Rachel related the story of a friend at Yale who was also her classmate in Israel. Although she lived on a single sex floor, the first time she took a shower she was confronted by a male student who entered her bathroom because his facility on the floor below was overcrowded. "Labels are relatively meaningless here because all floors are easily accessible to the opposite sex all hours of the day or night," said Rachel.

When she wrote to John Loge, the Dean of her Resident College, to express her concern that living in the dormitory would compromise her religious convictions, she also explained that she planned to get married at the end of December. He replied that Yale was not willing to bend on its policies. However, he recognized that she was an adult and that she could choose to live elsewhere as long as she paid for a dorm room. In the past Orthodox students have done just that, paying twice for living accommodations. This attitude is tantamount to "exacting a poll tax from people who want to observe and live according to their religious views," argued Rabbi Greer. "Yale doesn't have bed checks. They don't care whether these students are sleeping in their rooms."

Rachel agrees. "This is a type of *don't ask, don't tell policy*," she said. And while she has paid her tuition she has withheld payment for room and board and lives off campus. Rachel and her fiancée have decided to get married in a civil ceremony to satisfy the school's requirement. However, they plan to postpone living together until they have been officially married in a Jewish ceremony.

Therefore, the Yale 5 will soon become the Yale 4. "Even though I'm not actually a litigant in the case, I am involved because I believe we should not have to sacrifice our religious convictions for this new brand of morality or lack thereof," said Rachel. Alluding to Yale's preoccupation with the concept of diversity, she argued that "we have plenty of opportunities for interaction outside of the bedroom."

"This housing rule goes to the heart of the issue of diversity which Yale works so hard to promote," said Avi Hack, a graduate of Yale '97 and the brother of Elisha Hack. "Instead of giving lip service to the concept of diversity here is a situation where the university should allow students to be different on campus and live their lives according to their beliefs."

A View From The Dorm

Rabbi Michael Whitman, Rabbi of Young Israel of New Haven and Director of Young Israel House at Yale, acknowledged that the values and prohibitions concerning *Tznius* (modesty) are "way out of step with how many people feel today in our wider society. But religious Jews are bound to Biblical values, even when they are not currently in favor. The very definition of a Divine command is that it transcends contemporary popularity."

He concluded by suggesting that "the success of the Jewish family, for over three millennia, to preserve and nourish spiritual values, is ample testament to the benefits of this system – though for the religious Jew none are needed."

These remarks are contained in a lengthy e-mail that Rabbi Whitman sent to all Jewish students as well as to the two Yale newspapers. Now that the three thousand year-old rabbinical teachings regarding *Tznius* have taken up residence in cyberspace, perhaps Yale University will finally get the message also.

Epilogue:

Attorney Nathan Lewin filed suit on behalf of the Yale 5 contending that Yale's repeated denials of the students' requests violated their constitutional religious rights as well as antitrust law and the Fair Housing Act. The suit was dismissed on July 31, 1998 by U.S. District Judge Alfred V. Covello, who said that, "The plaintiffs could have opted to attend a different college or university if they were not satisfied with Yale's housing policy"

The students' appeal to the Second Circuit Court of Appeals ruled in favor of Yale in March 1999. In October 2001 the U.S. Supreme Court declined to take up the lawsuit and let stand the appeals court ruling that sided with Yale.

II

My Stay-at-Home Mom and the First Jewish Princess

*A*ndy Warhol would never have become famous if he had grown up in our house. There wasn't a soup can in sight because my mother prepared everything from scratch.

True, many people squeezed their own orange juice in those pre-Tropicana days, but how many made their own carrot juice? First, she grated each carrot by hand into a large white cotton handkerchief. Then she slowly and patiently proceeded to wring out the juice, drop by drop, until she filled up an entire glass.

In the morning, after we left for school, our stay-at-home-mom would navigate her shopping cart along Brighton Beach Avenue buying everything, from a freshly slaughtered chicken still bearing its feathers to a carp swimming in a shallow tub of water. When my brother Milton and I were lucky enough to tag along on these exploits, we would wander into the back of the butcher shop where we watched him "flick" the feathers off the chicken.

If my mother wasn't schlepping food up three flights of stairs, it was wet laundry. Although small items were washed by hand, once a week she hauled our bed sheets to a machine located two blocks from our home in the basement of an apartment building.

To save money on drying she brought the wet laundry back home where she hung it on the clothesline suspended outside our kitchen window. Once dry, then out came the ironing board. The word "idle" was not a part of my mother's vocabulary.

When I was growing up, my mother and my teachers were my role models. After I won the class spelling bee, Mrs. Carol Reilly, my third grade teacher at P.S. 100, presented me with my very first book, **Alice In Wonderland.** I fondly remember her as a beautiful and caring young woman whom I was eager to please. At the end of the school year, as a reward for my good grades, she cast me as the star in the play, **The Princess and the Rose-Colored Glasses.**

Since I didn't own a dress suitable for the role, Mrs. Reilly let me borrow the gown her little niece had worn to her wedding. Although the child was several years younger than me, because I was tiny, her dress fit perfectly. The day of the performance, dressed in my billowy yellow gown with lace bodice, I was transformed from a timid little refugee child into the member of a royal family. A shiny crown perched on my head, I made my entrance. Mrs. Reilly's niece, who was seated in the front row, exclaimed with delight so that the entire audience could hear, "Mommy, look! A princess is wearing my dress!"

I knew nothing about the original "Jewish princess" until I was an adult and began to read about our remarkable matriarchs. And so I finally came to understand that my mother's devotion to the care and feeding of her family was passed down via her DNA from an admirable ancestry, the ancient feminists, who continue to provide the role models that inform and guide the lives of modern Jewish women.

It began at the beginning with Sarah. Her name was originally Sarai, "my princess," which meant her claim to fame came from her role as Abraham's wife. However, according to our sages, G-d's covenant with our patriarch Abraham also included her, and so Sarai was changed to Sarah, "a princess to all the nations." The name change signified that she had become an equal partner with her husband and the ultimate role model.

A Taste of Shabbos

All of us are on our own personal journey and there are times we're not even aware that we've been traveling until we suddenly find ourselves at a new destination. My journey began unexpectedly when my husband and I were invited for Shabbos dinner at the home of his patients, Rabbi Zushe and Rebbetzin Esther Winner of the Seabreeze Jewish Center. As the pediatrician who took care of the couple's eight children, my husband already had a warm relationship with the family of Lubavitch Chassidim who welcomed Jews of all backgrounds to their home.

There were several other couples present, and although I found the conversation stimulating and the food extraordinary, it was the sheer joy of being Jewish that permeated the Winner home, which made the entire evening so unforgettable. That Friday night I discovered Shabbos was more than just chicken soup, an "aha" moment that led to a seismic shift in the direction of my life.

I started down this new path by enrolling in Esther's classes for women, tackling *Beginner's Hebrew and Beginner's Prayer,* so that unfamiliar words like *Hashem* gradually became a natural part of my vocabulary. Over the next few years we became good friends working closely together on several holiday programs, but it was the special taste of Shabbos I first experienced in her home that ultimately inspired me to produce a Jewish cooking video. Combining her expertise as an educator, gourmet cook and hostess with my expertise as a writer, *A Taste of Shabbos with Rebbetzin Esther Winner,* the video, was born.

As we developed the format the original concept grew and

it became more than just a cooking video. So, along with the fifteen recipes which included a six-braided challah, baked salmon a la Seabreeze and a chocolate cornucopia filled with rugelach, Esther explained the traditions that are so meaningful to the entire Shabbos experience. We also celebrated the sights and sounds of our hometown, Brooklyn, by filming on location in Brighton Beach, Coney Island, Williamsburg and Crown Heights.

Shortly after the video was released in 1994, I was contacted by the Joint Distribution Committee, who ordered a copy for their Jewish Cultural Center in Warsaw. My journey had come full circle. Fifty years after my parents were forced to flee Poland, their daughter brought a taste of Shabbos back to the home of her ancestors.

The video eventually begat a popular motivational seminar, *Life Is Like a Block of Chocolate*, which took us on the road and brought us into the homes and synagogues of women who represented the diversity of contemporary Jewish life. During a memorable trip to Los Angeles, we were introduced to Leah Adler, proprietor of the Milky Way Restaurant, who planned to show the video to her son, *the* Steven Spielberg. Esther and I never did hear from "the coast."

But as we traveled from Maine to Florida and New Jersey to California we did hear from a new generation of women who were eager to reconnect with their roots. After discussing the unique role of today's modern Jewish women, both in the home and in the workplace, Esther, aka the kosher Martha Stewart, presented a hands-on cooking demonstration of a recipe from our video and I shared the personal story of how I came to embrace Shabbos.

When I first decided to make myself *Shabbosdik*, I was thinking, who wouldn't want a day off from shopping and cooking and cleaning and writing and chauffeuring the kids around and answering the ever-ringing telephone, especially the cell. I became Shabbosdik by doing nothing. I didn't have to change my diet. I didn't have to change the way I dressed. I didn't have to change the way I wore my hair. On Shabbos all I had to do was nothing. A day about nothing. Sounds like a Seinfeld episode, but once your mind becomes Shabbosdik your heart and your soul follow. Shabbos was the beginning of the rest of my life.

Fool-Proof Parve Rugelach

Dough

4 sticks non-dairy margarine

6 cups flour

1 eight oz. container parve non-dairy whip topping

Filling

½ cup ground nuts

1 cup sugar

4 teaspoons cinnamon

1. Cream margarine in mixer.
2. Add flour and whip topping and mix for 2 minutes.
3. Divide dough into 6 equal parts and form into balls.
4. Refrigerate for one hour
5. Remove one ball at a time and roll out dough to ¼ inch thickness.
6. Spread filling over dough leaving ½ inch margin around border and 1 inch diameter circle in center of dough.
7. Cut into 16 equal slices with pie cutter or knife.
8. Starting from the outer edge of the dough roll each slice towards the center forming a crescent.
9. Bake on an ungreased cookie sheet for 15 minutes in a preheated 350 degree oven.

   Do not overbake. Tops of rugelach should remain light and the bottoms golden. Makes 96 rugelach.

In the Merit of Righteous Women

Turkey stuffed with kishke? Challah dipped in babaganoosh? Kugel? This was no ordinary Thanksgiving feast. In fact, everything about this meal was extraordinary: from the location, the private conference room of the Brooklyn District Attorney; the date, November 9, 1997, shortly after Succos, the holiday which had inspired the Pilgrim's original feast; the participants, a group of Orthodox Jewish and African-American women, and of course, the chefs.

Rebbetzin Esther Winner and I were invited to present our motivational seminar, *Life Is Like A Block Of Chocolate*, to the monthly meeting of **Mothers To Mothers**, a group that was created in the aftermath of the 1991 Crown Heights riots. Inspired by the Catholic and Protestant women in Northern Ireland, who were working together to achieve peace, Judge Charles Posner suggested to Henna White, the D.A.'s liaison to the Jewish community, and Jean Griffiths, whose son Michael had been killed in Howard Beach, that they attempt to do the same for their community. D.A. Charles J. Hynes generously volunteered his office as the common meeting ground and the rest is history.

"Everyone said it would never work, and then, when a core group of about twenty women began to meet regularly each month, everyone said it wouldn't last," said Henna White. Six years later, in addition to sharing close friendships, the women also share the honor of receiving the Anti-Defamation League's first *Heroes Against Hate Award* in recognition of their "singular achievements in building bridges in their community to fight hate."

Founded in 1913, the ADL's mission was "to stop the defamation of the Jewish people and to secure justice and fair treatment to all citizens alike." **Mothers To Mothers** represents what the ADL is all about, according to Jennifer Dann, Associate Director of the New York Regional Office. Now the ADL is encouraging this group to share what they have learned and take their message public.

And so we prepared a Thanksgiving feast in honor of what these "righteous" women had accomplished and presented each woman with a chocolate rose. But this celebration was just a "taste" of what awaited them. The next day a group composed of Henna White, Jean Griffiths, Sarah Himmelfarb, Viola Woods and Ann Lancaster, along with Judge Charles Posner, wife Lynn, and D.A. Hynes, were flown to Washington D.C. Their first stop was the Holocaust Museum.

"As we toured the museum," said Henna, "we were all very affected by what we saw. When we stood outside afterwards and talked about our reactions, everyone felt this experience had brought the group even closer together."

What followed next was a "most spectacular evening," according to Lynn Posner, a New York City public school teacher who had initially served as the facilitator for **Mothers To Mothers,** but eventually became an integral member of the group. Along with three other honorees, the women attended a dinner and *A Concert For Heroes* at the Kennedy Center for the Performing Arts where Maestro Leonard Slatkin conducted the National Symphony Orchestra. The evening, hosted by actors Ossie Davis and Ruby Dee, was organized by the ADL *"to honor the courage of ordinary men and women who have exposed injustice and protected others from the forces of hate and intolerance."*

"They called us heroes and gave us a standing ovation, but we felt we were just doing something that came naturally as women," said Henna White. The same sentiments were echoed by Lynn Posner, who insisted that "What we do is so simple, it's extraordinary in its ordinariness. The problem is that more people don't do it."

Ann Lancaster, Chairperson of the 71st Precinct Council, noted that her participation in the group had provided her with a better understanding of the Orthodox culture, which she was then able to share with her own community.

"If a hero saves a life," said Henna White, "then I suppose in our own way, we contributed to saving a community." The evening culminated with a spontaneous midnight visit to the Lincoln Memorial where **Mothers To Mothers** rededicated themselves to the "ordinary" work they were doing.

Fran Sheldon:
The World Is Her Stage

The news director searched through the contents of the newly arrived gift basket, carefully examining each item. He approached this latest task with the same intense scrutiny that he reserved for all his important assignments. Finally, his efforts paid off as he held up a box of chocolates and triumphantly announced, "The wrapper on this one has an 'O' with a little 'u' in it. Fran can eat it!"

Every day, quietly and without fanfare, newswoman Fran Sheldon goes about her job at WINS Radio, not intending to alter the workplace, but she does.

As a child she was stricken with the acting bug and dreamt of a life on the stage. However, Fran's mother, a teacher at a local Yeshiva, and her father, an electrical engineer, were concerned about the precarious nature of a career in the theater and suggested she direct her efforts toward a more acceptable field. When Fran received a Degree in Communications from Queens College, who could have predicted that one day she would reach an audience that numbers in the millions?

All The News All The Time

A graduate of Bais Yaakov Academy of Queens and Shevach High School, the little girl who aspired to be an actress went on to acquire an impressive resume. While still in high school, she approached Soshia Leibler, an Orthodox woman working in news radio, who helped her land her first internship with WOR Radio in 1987. A summer job as an associate producer at WMCA followed. While still in college, Fran worked as a per diem news production assistant at WINS Radio, "the most listened to news station in the nation."

After graduation she continued working at WINS, while also freelancing at ABC Talk Radio, Daynet and NBC Talknet. She produced several call-in talk shows for a noteworthy roster of celebrities, including Alan Colmes, Bob Brinker and Ralph Snodsmith. Barry Farber, she discovered, "was a brilliant man who speaks thirteen languages fluently," and was easy to work with. Screening calls for Sally Jessy Raphael and making sure her radio program ran smoothly was also a gratifying experience.

A full-time position at WINS was offered to her in 1993 and Fran was promoted to the prestigious job of full-time Service Aide in 1996 with a steady writing shift and position as Editor. "The Editor," Fran explained, "is presented with a blank sheet of paper and is responsible for writing the entire news show." Working with the Pack File, which combines information from the editors, reporters and wire services that pour into the newsroom twenty-four hours a day from all over the world, Fran had ninety minutes to put together a one hour program. And throughout the day she continually had to update the latest stories. When a big story broke she had to write it "in a minute" and sometimes under the most daunting circumstances.

Dealing With Disaster

"The day that the 1993 Word Trade Center bombing suspects were arrested I was at my desk even though it was a Fast day, *Tanis Esther*," she pointed out. "I had planned to leave work by 4:30 to be home in time to hear the Megillah reading at 7 p.m." The News Director was impressed with her zeal, but concerned about her decision to continue working.

"I can't believe you agreed to work overtime when you're fasting," he told her. A job in the news field, Fran has learned, demands a lot of flexibility.

"Once during a storm," she recounted, "I was snowed in at

work for two days and couldn't get home, so WINS had to put me up in a hotel."

She is especially proud of her station's coverage of the 1999 Hurricane Floyd disaster. "While I was planning the program, I tried to keep in mind what I as a listener would want to hear," said Fran. "In order to reassure the public and brief them on what was being done, I arranged to have an official from the state or the city government on the air every hour." Her frequent contact with the mayor left a positive impression. "I have interviewed Mayor Giuliani several times and I found him very different from other public officials, especially since he makes a genuine effort to remember your name," she said.

The Secret of Success

What kind of rating does she give to WINS? "It's an incredible place to work. Management is extremely supportive and very sensitive." She goes on to reveal that, "before I was hired I made it very clear that I was an observant Jew and therefore had specific requirements in terms of my work schedule." In addition to Jewish holidays, Fran's major concern was leaving work at 3 p.m. on Fridays in the winter in order to make it home before Shabbos. "They assured me that they would work out a suitable schedule for me and true to their word they did. I now work Sunday through Thursday."

Not only did Steve, her News Director, hasten to remind her one year that she had forgotten to put in her request to take off on Yom Kippur, but, Fran chuckled, he's probably the only Wasp who has Purim circled on his calendar. "He looks forward to my home-baked hamantashen every year." It was also Steve who scrupulously checked out the contents of a gift food basket the station received recently looking for items that were okay for Fran to eat. She is especially appreciative of the station's respect for her dietary requirements, explaining that whenever the staff orders in, they thoughtfully provide a special kosher meal for her.

A Majority of One

Fran credits her father's sound advice with contributing to

her success as an Orthodox woman in the workplace.

"I realize that in my job I have a tremendous responsibility being one of the few Orthodox Jews that many non-Jews come into contact with," Fran noted. For instance, because she owns several wigs, "sometimes my hair is straight and sometimes it's curly. New people at WINS are always surprised by the dramatic change in my appearance and can't figure out how I can look so different from one day to the next." A co-worker who comes from a tiny town in Illinois once told Fran, "you are the only person like you that I have ever met." They ultimately struck up a friendship so that she feels comfortable talking to Fran about Judaism. "I know I can always come to you and get answers to all these questions that I have," she confided.

In addition to her credentials as a responsible newswoman, there have been other advantages to Fran's presence in the newsroom. For example, during the 1999 Israeli election, when Netanyahu gave his concession speech in Hebrew, Fran was able to translate it immediately so that WINS was the first station on the air in the tri-state area with news of the speech. Does she ever find a conflict between the way the media portrays Israel and her news editing? "If I do, I say something. But often it's a case of the media just merely repeating what they have picked up from the wire service," said Fran. To illustrate, she cites the time the wire copy erroneously referred to Israel's "occupied territories."

Ari's Favorite Story

Another example of Fran's unique contribution to the workplace also turns out to be her husband Ari's favorite news story. A reporter who had been sent to cover the basketball playoffs called the station and demanded to be put through immediately to Fran. "I know absolutely nothing about sports and everyone at the station knows that, so they thought the reporter must be mistaken," Fran said. "But he kept insisting, 'I must talk to Fran.'

"When I finally picked up the phone, the reporter, whose name is Anthony, told me that he just interviewed a guy and wanted to know if he could put the interview on the air. But, I protested, I don't know anything about sports. 'Please, Fran,'

Anthony pleaded, 'just listen to the tape and tell me if he's cursing.' Intrigued, I heard Anthony ask the man if he was a Knicks fan. He enthusiastically answered yes. But when Anthony asked him what would happen if the Knicks lost, I could hear the man gasp, "*Chas v'sholom*, the Knicks can't lose!"

The Knicks didn't win after all. They were beaten by Houston, but millions of people heard a Hebrew prayer drift over the airwaves one afternoon because Fran Sheldon was at the Editor's Desk.

Livia Bitton-Jackson: Recipient of the Emunah Jewish Heritage Award

Each of us has a pasuk, a line in the Torah which corresponds to our name. My Hebrew name is 'Leah' and so my pasuk begins with a lamed and ends with a heh. When I was a young child I learned that my pasuk meant I would live to tell about the acts of G-d. Because I knew my pasuk, I knew I would not die when I was sent to Auschwitz."

For young Leah Friedman who grew up in a small town near Bratislav, Czechoslovakia, there was no formal Jewish education. It was an environment where religion was just "empty ritual" for a girl. But her life and her relationship to Judaism changed forever when she was thirteen years old and she and her mother were sent to the Nazi death camp.

"If I was being persecuted for being a Jew, I wanted to know why. I wanted to learn, what is a Jew?" This startling revelation comes from Livia Bitton-Jackson, a Professor of Judaic Studies, a renowned historian and an award-winning author of works on Jewish subjects.

"After my liberation in 1945 I considered it my personal mission to carry on and speak of the ways of G-d. And so I have dedicated my entire life to teaching," Mrs. Jackson said. Livia began with the little children in the displaced persons camps in Germany where she worked as an interpreter for the International Refugee Organization (IRO) in 1949.

She and her mother emigrated to America in 1951 and were

reunited with her brother, Armin Friedman, who went on to become the principal of the Hebrew Academy of Long Beach and a Professor of Talmud at Yeshiva University. She pursued her studies, earning a Masters Degree in Hebrew Culture and a PhD in Jewish History from NYU.

After teaching Hebrew at Brooklyn College and other universities here and abroad, she became the head of the Department of Hebraic and Judaic Studies at the Herbert H. Lehman College of CCNY.

She has continued her teaching outside the classroom as an enthusiastic spokeswoman for Emunah. "My raison d'etre, the reason I work for Emunah is to impart *Yiddishkeit*. By speaking about the accomplishments of these talented religious women, I do my share to contribute to the future of the Jewish people on a grass roots level."

With more than 225 schools and action centers in 150 communities throughout Israel, Emunah affects every aspect of Jewish life: from the College of Arts and Technology for Young Women in Jerusalem to the Golden Age Center for senior citizens in Petach Tikvah and the Ulpanim and Ulpaniot for new immigrants, Emunah's influence reaches far into the fields of health, education and social welfare.

In recognition of their devotion to the state of Israel and their dedication to the work of Emunah, Livia and her husband, Dr. Leonard Jackson, were honored with the Jewish Heritage Award at the 1994 Emunah Women's Diamond Key Dinner at the Marriott Marquis Hotel.

Dr. Jackson, a specialist in internal and family medicine, was born in Ireland and received his education and medical training in England. During WWII, when he was a young intern in London, he volunteered for the British armed forces to help liberate his fellow Jews from the Nazis. After the war he participated in Zionist activities in England to bring about the establishment of the state of Israel. Then, as a young doctor, he went to Israel to make a tangible contribution by helping develop the country's outpatient hospital services.

Livia is generous with her praise for her husband. She said,

"If it weren't for Len's enthusiastic support for all my endeavors, I couldn't have accomplished all that I have. He encouraged me to go to Kenya to cover the United Nations End of the Decade of the Woman Conference for the Jewish Press. He is always at my side."

Married in Dublin 18 years ago, the couple has a *ketubah* written in Hebrew and Gaelic. Livia and Leonard realized a cherished dream by ultimately making their home in Israel. He is an attending physician at Laniado Hospital in Netanya. Livia is currently Professor of History at Tel Aviv University in Ramat Aviv.

Livia has chronicled her own journey in her memoir, *Elli: Coming of Age in the Holocaust,* which received the 1982 Jewish Heritage Award from the Association of Orthodox Teachers (Philadelphia Chapter) as well as the 1981 Christopher Award, a prize for books that affirm the highest qualities of the human spirit. The life this elegant and accomplished woman has chosen to lead is a reflection of her deep respect for her heritage, her love for her people and her profound faith in the ways of G-d.

Sharsheret: The Missing Link

After setting goals for ourselves, carefully mapping out the direction and destination of our lives, we are often confronted by a detour that presents us with a completely new set of challenges.

A Phi Beta Kappa graduate of Barnard with a Law degree from Columbia University, where she served as editor of the Law Review, Rochelle Shoretz was a rising star in the legal profession. And then at the age of 28, the direction of her life underwent a dramatic shift. "I found a lump."

"When I was first diagnosed with breast cancer I was desperately seeking someone to talk to. Friends called and volunteered their mothers or their grandmothers, but I really felt I needed to speak to a woman my own age with a common life experience."

However, when Mrs. Shoretz called cancer support organizations, she was often paired with women who were at the same stage of treatment or shared the same diagnosis, but otherwise had absolutely nothing in common with her. "What I needed was someone to talk to about the issues that affected my daily life as a young Orthodox Jewish woman with a husband and two small children. But if you are paired with someone who needs a whole introduction to Judaism or your particular lifestyle, it can make for an awkward conversation."

She had trouble finding someone until a mutual friend introduced her to Lauryn Weiser, another young Jewish woman recently diagnosed with breast cancer and now a Sharsheret volunteer. "It has made all the difference in my treatment. I turned to her for support and guidance."

Mrs. Shoretz's own experience convinced her that the needs of young Jewish women with breast cancer was a neglected area in the realm of cancer support. A take-charge type of person, she was determined to provide the missing link.

"*Sharsheret* is Hebrew for chain and I envisioned women united in experience and strengthened by one another as links in a chain." She emphasized that Sharsheret is for *all* Jewish women, Orthodox, Reform, Conservative or unaffiliated. "We're reaching out to single women, married women, women with and without children. Our goal is to match people based not only on similar medical diagnoses, but also on common life experience."

Although Sharsheret has been a daunting undertaking, she has been overwhelmed by the positive response since it was founded in 2001. "To be part of something new and exciting is very energizing. We have almost an equal mix of women who are calling us asking for support and women calling to be supporters." She finds the strength and commitment of the young women in the Jewish community particularly heartening. "These are women who are themselves going through chemotherapy or struggling to deal with their own medical issues. But they are taking time out from their extremely busy schedules to help others because they understand what it's like."

Volunteers may be living with cancer themselves or just want to be supportive, like Sara Rudoff Olshin, a young married woman with children who volunteers as Director of Public Relations. When Mrs. Shoretz told her close friend about her plans for Sharsheret, Sara's immediate response was, "I'm on board, what can I do?" She added that, "Rochie has the right balance of professionalism and sensitivity and she has energized all the volunteers. Her dynamic personality and her sincerity and vision is the driving force behind Sharsheret." Where did this sense of purpose come from?

Rochelle grew up in the Midwood section of Brooklyn where she was "surrounded by very strong female role models who had a significant impact on my life." She is especially grateful to her mother, Sherry Tenenbaum, a special education teacher. She is also indebted to Carol Shoretz, her stepmother, and Dr. Susan Katz, the principal of Shulamith High School. "These women were there for me as role models and have been there for me as supporters as well." She was honored by her alma mater with the school's first *Alumnus of the Year Award* at their annual dinner in 2002.

Always the legal eagle, she insists on being very clear about Sharsheret's mission. "We're not a referral service and it's not an organization meant to give out medical advice. It's an organization where women can share their experiences and all conversations are confidential," she stresses. "If women are seeking medical guidance, we can refer them to specific organizations that are staffed and trained to deal with their questions."

Sharsheret is also not a support group. There are many such well-run groups already in existence all over the tri-state area and nationally; however, she learned from personal experience that this type of group has its drawbacks.

"I found it very difficult to make time to attend meetings when you're so busy living with cancer." She observed that some of the women who call Sharsheret are struggling to raise their children, continue with their careers and keep all their medical appointments. "To ask them to give up more time by leaving the house and attending meetings under these straining conditions can be very difficult, whereas two women can coordinate a schedule easier than ten women." She suggested that, "Picking up the telephone and calling somebody when you need to talk makes things easier and I wanted women to be able to connect that way."

This is precisely how Mrs. Shoretz connected with Chana, the mother of five, who was searching for answers. One day the phone rang and "Rochie was there for me. She knew what lay ahead for me because she was already further down the road in her treatment," Chana noted. A Sharsheret supporter can offer the kind of invaluable advice that family and friends may be unable to. "A best friend can sympathize with you but can't really understand what you're going through," said Chana, who is today a volunteer supporting someone else who's just starting down the familiar road she's already traveled.

Mrs. Shoretz points out that there are many Jewish organizations doing extremely beneficial work in heightening awareness of breast cancer and the importance of early detection. But where do women go once they've been diagnosed and begun treatment? "Interest in Sharsheret is snowballing precisely because we're filling this void." She is gratified that Sharsheret has been contacted by the American Cancer Society, which is excited to have an organization dealing specifically with issues facing young Jewish women with breast cancer such as the increased risk for Ashkenazi women; issues related to child rearing, child bearing, marital purity and the role of religion in life with cancer.

"I would like *Sharsheret* to become a place for women to talk about the role of Judaism in their lives whatever that role might be, whether it's an increased desire to learn about their religion or to cope with being a religious person in crisis." She hopes that whether you find comfort in Judaism or you're struggling with religious issues, Sharsheret links will find it beneficial to talk to each other about these issues. "I get the most beautiful letters from women I don't even know who have heard about Sharsheret," says its founder "and are touched by the work that so many of our volunteers are doing."

Epilogue:

In 2007 Rochelle Shoretz and Sharsheret each celebrated a significant anniversary. It had been five years since Rochelle was first diagnosed and then, along with her dedicated team, went on to create this innovative support network for other women newly diagnosed with breast cancer. In these five years Sharsheret has responded to more than 10,000 phone calls; welcomed more than 400 participants from 31 states to the Link program; published and distributed over 60,000 educational booklets, and launched an online message board at www.sharsheret.org and succeeeded in connecting, educating and supporting Jewish women and their families facing breast cancer.

Molly Finkel: A Lady of Firsts

When I entered the home of Molly Finkel, a gentle, charming woman whose remarkable association with Emunah reads like the history of the twentieth century, I was greeted by a wall covered with tributes. Among the numerous plaques engraved with words of gratitude and praise, there was one in particular which summed up her achievements as the "matriarch of a family of generations committed to the furtherance and enhancement of our sacred House of Torah."

Born in 1910 in Savran, a small Ukrainian town, Malka Berdichefsky related the story of how she came to be raised in two homes. Growing up in czarist Russia, she learned at an early age that a Jew's daily existence was in constant peril. Her beloved father, Kalman, who was the rabbi of the town, was tragically killed by Cossacks during the 1919 revolution.

The family immigrated to America after her mother remarried Osher Zelek Finkel, the chief rabbi of Odessa. Molly's intellectual curiosity and love of Torah were nurtured in a home where scholars gathered to talk politics and culture. "I would stay up late at night listening to them argue and debate," she recalls with nostalgia.

This stimulating environment compelled her to join the religious Zionist organization, Hapoel Hamizrahi, whose meetings were attended by both men and women. When Rabbi Herzog of Jerusalem came to address the group in the early 1930s, he lamented the deplorable educational conditions in Israel. It was at this crucial meeting that the women accepted the challenge to provide all Jewish children with a quality education.

To achieve this goal, Molly helped found Hapoel Hamizrahi Women, which ultimately became known worldwide as the influential social service organization, Emunah. As a result of its continued commitment to Israel, under the leadership of dedicated women like Molly, *Emunah* has created an incredible network of schools, hospitals and senior centers, which have had a powerful effect on the lives of Israelis, young and old.

"When I made up my mind that this was the organization I wanted to work for, I devoted all my energy to their programs. But Emunah did more for me than I did for Emunah. It helped build my character. Emunah made me realize that there were so many opportunities to help people. We would pick the poorest projects in Israel and support them. In the beginning I walked around 42nd Street with a *pushka* in my hand."

A top priority was providing bed linens for the schools in Israel. To accomplish this Molly held parties in her home in East New York that were the forerunners of the modern fundraiser. "My mother baked knishes and you were admitted to the party only if you came with a donation of linens which we packed up and shipped off to Israel."

Molly's mother had the proud distinction of being the first Life Member of Emunah. "When I finally had the opportunity to visit the nurseries and kindergartens in Israel, I felt enormous gratification for what Emunah had accomplished." She had the privilege of meeting Prime Minister Menachem Begin when he dedicated the Emunah nursery in Efrat in her honor.

Molly grew up in what she described as a "house of principle" where she formed her ideals and also met the person who was to become her husband of 40 years, her step-brother Shmuel Finkel. She helped him first through New York Law School and then to become a rabbi. Molly recounted the story of how a visitor from Kansas City was so impressed when he heard young Rabbi Finkel address his congregation in New Haven, Connecticut that he insisted he become the rabbi of his synagogue in Missouri.

The couple arrived in Kansas City in 1941 at a time when

the city's Jewish doctors were not permitted to work in the local hospital. Molly responded with typical determination, "Let's build our own!" Because of her vision and efforts, Kansas City opened the first strictly kosher Jewish hospital in Missouri.

She was also the first to open her home to boys in the military who were stationed far from home. "This was the only opportunity many of them ever had to observe Shabbos." Years later she was gratified to learn that, because of their inspiring experiences in her home, several of these boys became religious.

Molly and her husband returned to New York when her father-in-law became ill and Rabbi Finkel took over his congregation on Blake Avenue in Brooklyn. Eventually the family made their home in Belle Harbor, Queens and Shmuel Finkel practiced law full time, developing a reputation as a prominent attorney. Molly's two sons have continued the tradition of their late father. Kalman Finkel was appointed Commissioner of the NYC Housing Authority by Mayor Rudolph Giuliani. His brother, Osher Finkel, became an attorney for the Legal Aid Society.

During her lifelong association with Emunah, Molly served on the Board of National Emunah and she was instrumental in founding three chapters, Rishona in Brownsville, Daroma in Far Rockaway and Yerushalayim in Belle Harbor. She served in many capacities on the national level, including co-editorship of the *Menorah Bulletin* which she established.

As she looked back on a life devoted to fulfilling the needs of her community, supporting *Vaad Hatzola,* yeshivot and hospitals, she derived immense satisfaction from the contributions she has made.

Molly Finkel's children, grandchildren, great-grandchildren and the generations of Israeli children she helped are the awesome legacy of this inspiring woman.

"Where Have You Come From and Where Are You Going?"

W e're not here to burn our *sheitels*," announced Dr. Adena Berkowitz. Of course she was speaking metaphorically, because this attorney, wife and mother wasn't wearing a head covering and neither were most of the 2000 participants she addressed at the Third International Conference On Feminism and Orthodoxy.

A survey of the audience seated in the grand ballroom of the Grand Hyatt quickly dispelled any preconceived notions of what an Orthodox Feminist looked like, as grandmothers with close-cropped hairdos and young women sporting baseball caps and infant carriers were seated among men with beards and men without. A luxury hotel in mid-town Manhattan seemed like an incongruous setting for discussing the finer points of *Halacha* and yet here we were, linen napkins on our laps and poached salmon on our plates, debating a 3000 year old legacy.

The intriguing title of the conference, **"Where Have You Come From And Where Are You Going?"** was taken from the question the angel posed to *Hagar* in order to "give her the opportunity to reflect on her own predicament," according to Belda Lindenbaum, the Vice President of the Jewish Orthodox Feminist Alliance (JOFA). A resource, advocacy and educational organization founded in 1998, JOFA's goal is to upgrade and enhance the roles and responsibilities of women in Orthodox Judaism by sponsoring a conference such as this which seeks to expand the spiritual, ritual, intellectual and political opportunities for women within the framework of Halacha.

"We come from empty benches in synagogues," continued Mrs. Lindenbaum, the co-founder with her husband and Rabbi Shlomo Riskin of Midreshet Lindenbaum in Jerusalem. "We come from Miriam the prophet, Deborah the judge and Yael the warrior . . .and we're going toward a new fresh reading of the texts," said the woman who has defined herself as an Orthodox Feminist for over twenty-five years. "For me it means equality of opportunity and equality of dignity."

The question "Where Have You Come From And Where Are You Going?" became a familiar refrain during the two-day conference encouraging me to reflect on my own feminist journey. Back in the sixties, when the National Organization of Women was in its infancy, I attended a NOW meeting, but walked out, never to return, when a woman twenty years my senior revealed she had left her husband because he wouldn't let her get a job. I was a young bride who had just graduated college. Working for an advertising agency and putting my husband through medical school, I was already living the feminism that the women of NOW were seeking.

Dr. Sylvia Barack Fishman, Co-Director, International Research Institute on Jewish Women at Brandeis University, recognized a similar gap at the conference when she acknowledged that since younger Jewish women are more thoroughly educated than their mothers, many viewed feminism as "so sixties." Young women I spoke with, like Leora Nathan, were already attending tefilla groups and took their feminism in stride.

"Orthodox Jewish women expect our lives to have coherence. We expect to be able to use our minds and energies in our Jewish lives as well as our secular lives," said Dr. Fishman. With impressive credentials in hand, these CEOs and university professors and legal eagles expect the equal rights they enjoy in the workplace to translate into equal rights in the prayer place. It's not surprising, therefore, that they refuse to be relegated to the back of the shul.

Blu Greenberg, the President and founder of JOFA, firmly

believes that "Torah is the source of all ethical values but Torah comes from heaven, it doesn't reside in heaven." She went on to affirm that establishing the full dignity and participation of women within Jewish law is a historical and religious necessity. "How Orthodoxy will resolve women's issues in the next century will be a touchstone of its credibility and vitality."

And so for two days, in more than 50 workshops and lectures, we discussed the plight of the *agunot*, family violence in the Jewish community, widowed and divorced women, single motherhood by choice, dress as a reflection of gender roles, women's Talmud study and women reciting kaddish. However, when author Haviva Ner-David revealed that she held an *upsheren* for her daughter, when the child turned three and presented her with her own *tsitsit*, it was obvious to me that many of these women were still defining themselves by emulating men.

And although speaker after speaker reaffirmed a love of Torah and a devotion to *Halacha*, a central figure was conspicuously missing from much of the discourse. With the emphasis on personal fulfillment, was anyone serving *Hashem* at this table?

"When you don't know where you're going, any road will take you there," noted Rabbi Irving Greenberg, co-founder of CLAL, the National Jewish Center for Learning and Leadership. "We cannot apply Halacha properly unless we know where we're going," he continued during his talk on *A Feminist Orthodox Reading of the Tradition*. "Our task as religious Jews is to become a partner with the creator to complete and perfect the world." Because women in the Orthodox community don't have all the rights they have everywhere else, "Figure out how you can do it Halachically," he suggested.

"This conference and the quest of Orthodox Feminists is all about the quest for the almighty," said Rabbi Avi Weiss, spiritual leader of the Hebrew Institute of Riverdale, the first synagogue to house a women's prayer group because they recognized "the yearning of women to feel G-d's presence."

He went on to point out in his lecture, *Women Finding G-d in Prayer and Torah*, that the real message of Torah is that "Avraham and Sarah were given the mandate to bring G-d back into the world."

During the beginning of the last century, G-d's presence was observed mainly in the small *shtetels* across Eastern Europe. At the dawn of the 21st century, when 2000 people convene in the most powerful city in the world for the purpose of discussing and debating the different paths to Orthodox Judaism, we are bearing witness to a miracle.

III

The Chicken Farm, The Doug-lass and the Blind Date

I was fourteen years old the summer my mother decided we needed a dose of fresh country air. For her that meant New Jersey. All it took was a phone call and we were off to visit Jake's chicken farm. My mother and Jacob Finkelstein had grown up together in a Polish shtetel called Uchanie. Like the other remaining townspeople who had survived the Holocaust, Jake and his wife immigrated to America, but instead of following their "landsman" to the city they opted to raise a brood of chickens and children on White Horse Pike in Atco, New Jersey.

The oldest daughter, Debbie, was my age and we became immediate friends. My younger brother Milton found a pal in Sol, the only son. The two youngest girls, Pauline and Barbara, were like the little sisters I never had.

By the end of our week's stay the bond between Debbie and me had become firmly established. Our friendship thrived during our high school years as we corresponded by mail and maintained a city mouse, country mouse type of relationship. During winter break, when Debbie came to visit, we went to Manhattan to see "West Side Story." Summer vacation brought me back to the farm and an excursion to

Atlantic City.

While many of my classmates at Lincoln High School were busy making plans for college, I readily understood that going out of town was not an option for me. Brooklyn College was a short bus ride away and each afternoon I returned to the safety and sameness of home.

Debbie, however, went confidently off to Douglass College, the all girls sister school of Rutgers University. Her freedom became my ticket to the world beyond Brooklyn. Each semester I boarded the bus at the Port Authority Terminal in Manhattan and headed for New Brunswick, New Jersey, where for one entire weekend I adopted the persona of a coed living in a dorm, embracing campus life.

My final trip almost didn't take place. Distressed by a sudden ear infection, I cancelled my plans, but at the very last minute decided to go after all. This was senior year and I didn't want to pass up the opportunity to spend my final weekend on campus. When Debbie heard I was coming, she phoned her date Paul, a medical student, and suggested he ask his roommate to join us. He wasn't available.

Luck? Fate? Destiny? Where Jews are concerned no matter what happens it's always bashert. Walking down the hallway, wondering how he was going to solve this dating conundrum, Paul bumped into Richard, a fellow classmate who was free for the evening. The four of us went to see a newly released movie called **The Graduate.** *The film became a classic and my date became my husband. A lifetime later, another fateful encounter – our oldest son Joshua was introduced to Paul's former roommate at Lenox Hill Hospital where today they are both colleagues.*

When Joshua decided to follow in his father's footsteps, my husband hoped that would ultimately lead him to his Pediatric office in Brooklyn. However, Joshua chose another path. Today, he is a board-certified Nephrologist in private practice in Manhattan, a Clinical Assistant Professor of Medicine at New York University School of Medicine and a Clinical Instructor of Medicine at Columbia University College of Physicians and Surgeons.

The Graduate

The birth of a child is a blessing for any family, but for our family my son Joshua's birth was also an affirmation. He was the first child to be born a citizen of the United States of America to a family whose personal history was marked by pogroms, labor camps and displaced persons camps, the legacy of persecution. We gave Joshua the yiddish name, Yankif Yossel, in memory of his great-great-grandfather at the request of my father, David.

Although he was reluctant to talk about his painful past, my father often spoke of that memorable day when Yankif Yossel gathered the large Zejerman family together in the small Polish town of Sarnaki. A wise and righteous man, Yankif Yossel realized that war was imminent, but he was too old to fight and too frail to leave, so he blessed each member of the family, said good-bye, closed his eyes and died. He was 104 years old.

My father's family were expert cabinetmakers who constructed most of the buildings and furniture in Sarnaki, though in his youth my father also studied to become a rabbi. The war forced him to become a student of survival as well. He was the sole member of his immediate family to survive the Holocaust. My mother, Devorah, was more fortunate. She had her brother, Moishe Berger. With their family murdered and their town of Uchanie destroyed, it was only their devotion to each other that sustained Moishe and Devorah and enabled them to endure and overcome unimaginable hardships during the nightmare that followed.

For many who were left homeless and orphaned, the war was the *shatran* – the matchmaker – who brought couples together. And so, miraculously, the victims of a cruelty beyond comprehension managed to find the strength to marry and create new lives and new families. My brother Milton and I were born while our parents languished in various displaced person's camps in Germany. Immigration quotas kept us in limbo for several years, citizens of nowhere, until we were finally permitted to immigrate to America in 1951.

The Hebrew Immigrant Aid Society (HIAS) found us a home in a clapboard boarding house in Brooklyn, on West 2nd Street, on the edge of Coney Island. As my family prospered we moved to a tenement on West 3rd Street, opposite P.S. 100. When I started kindergarten, *"ich obe giret bloyze Yiddish"* (I spoke only Yiddish). But by the end of the year I had a new language and a new name. The school dentist had suggested to my parents that they give me and my brother names more appropriate for an American child. And so Mordecai, (named for our maternal grandfather) was renamed Milton after a popular '50s television entertainer. And Chaya became Helen. When we officially became American citizens in 1956, my parents changed the spelling of their last name from the Polish Zejerman to Zegerman which was easier to pronounce.

My father took advantage of the opportunities here using his ingenuity and his craftsman's skills to rebuild his life by rebuilding Brooklyn. With his golden hands he was capable of constructing a tiny cradle for my doll, and years later a large home for my growing family. When he was well into his seventies, my father finally revealed to me that he deeply regretted that he was unable to continue his education and become a surgeon.

My father-in-law, Abraham Schwimmer, also aspired to be a doctor. In the 1930s, when religious quotas kept him from receiving a medical education here, he attempted to attend medical school in Europe. But the threat of war brought him back home where he became a pharmacist instead. And so along with the antibiotics and the cold remedies, he also dispensed a generous dose of TLC to anyone who walked through the door of the Prospect Pharmacy in Garfield, New Jersey.

Joshua's grandfathers were not present to see him fulfill his dreams and theirs. But his grandmothers, Frieda Wiland Schwimmer and Dora Berger Zegerman, were seated in the audience the day that their children's child was awarded his MD degree from the University of Rochester School of Medicine. As he descended from the stage of the Eastman Theater, Yankif Yossel cradled in his very capable hands a single sheaf of paper that spoke volumes.

. The Saving Remnant

Would you like to see the room where you were born?"
I looked into the earnest face of Pater Conrad, the elderly
Benedictine monk who had been selected to take me on a tour of
the St. Ottilien Monastery.

"You know which room it is?" I asked him haltingly.

"Yes, sure." he said in a heavy German accent. "Please follow
me upstairs."

As we slowly ascended the wide staircase I visualized my
mother walking up these very stairs, grasping the same heavy
wooden railing for support. When we reached the landing, he
turned left and I followed him down to the end of the hallway. We
stopped in front of room 150.

"This was the birthing room," said Pater Conrad as he
turned the knob and pushed open the door to my past.

I was born in the St. Ottilien DP camp hospital while my
parents, who came from small towns in Poland, were waiting for
permission to immigrate to Israel or the United States or anyplace
that would have us. When I was three years old, we finally set sail
for America. On the eve of my fiftieth birthday I returned to my
birthplace seeking the answers to a lifetime of questions. For me
the Holocaust was like a giant question mark that cast its long,
dark shadow over my entire life which began at St. Ottilien.

The DP Experience
This need to comprehend compelled me once again to

make another journey several years later to attend "Life Reborn: Jewish Displaced Persons 1945-1951." The four-day conference had been organized by the Second Generation Advisory Group and the U.S. Holocaust Memorial Museum in association with the American Joint Distribution Committee. Accompanied by my husband and my son, Andrew, we joined over one thousand survivors, their families, former military personnel and historians who converged on Washington, D.C. in January 2000 to focus on the extraordinary lives of the uprooted and homeless people classified as displaced persons.

We pinned on identification badges which carried the names Landsberg, Fohrenwald and Eshwege, the DP camps we had lived in, and then spent the next four days scanning each other's IDs. We were the alumni of a strange and yet uplifting reunion. I had come determined to connect with anyone who had anything to do with St. Ottilien. I didn't have to wait long.

As I sat in the hotel and searched the database provided by the U.S. Holocaust Museum, the picture of an attractive young woman named Henia Durmashkin appeared on my computer screen. Her bio explained that she had been the member of a distinguished musical family originally from Vilna. Henia had been liberated on a death march from Dachau and joined the newly formed St. Ottilien Orchestra which played throughout the U.S. and British zones in Germany. Two days later I attended a panel discussion on artistic creativity in the DP camps and listened, mesmerized, as Henia Durmashkin told us her story.

The Second Generation

"There is no place in the world where so many stories are accumulated under one roof," said Elie Wiesel, who delivered the keynote address at the conference. "Every one of you has a story, every story deserves to be told and every life is for all of us a miracle if you accept that there were miracles in those times."

Professor Wiesel went on to relate the painful story that one of his students shared with him. His father, the student revealed, had been married before the war but his wife and children were killed. His mother had been married as well and her husband

and children were also killed. His parents met in a DP camp. He is their son, but "whenever they look at me, they don't see me," said the young man. This was familiar terrain.

During the 1960s our generation was in the throes of an identity crisis, frivolously trying to find themselves. But for the children of Holocaust survivors, our identity had always eluded us because we were never sure who it was our parents saw when they looked at us. Sometimes we were their little brothers and sisters, the *tyere kinderlach,* who never grew up, and as we got older, we became their mothers and fathers whose names we carried.

Like second hand smoke, the fumes from the ovens had permeated our core, forever altering our perception of the world and ourselves. We were identified as the children of survivors. but as we went on to have children and grandchildren of our own we became the second generation and then simply 2G. Although our parents had been displaced in time and space, they knew who they were because they carried their Jewishness in their very sinews along with the memories of their loved ones, their *shtetels,* their Shabbats.

Shabbat. A handful of us gathered for services in one of the hotel meeting rooms. As the rich voices of Cantor Moshe Kraus, cantor of the Bergen-Belsen DP camp, and Cantor Isaac Goodfriend, choir member the Feldafing DP camp, drifted over the make-shift *mechitza,* I felt an odd sense of camaraderie to the women *davening* alongside me. And as we raised our voices, each prayer was an affirmation of our decision to lead meaningful Jewish lives.

Outside the hotel, buses waited to take conference participants to the Holocaust Memorial Museum to view the remnants and the fragments of a once thriving civilization. The irony didn't escape me. For those outside Judaism was defined by treasured artifacts and relics buried in concrete and steel. For those of us who remained inside it defined our life.

Sh'erit ha-Pletah

When elected delegates of survivors met in Munich in 1946 they officially called themselves the *Sh'erit ha-Pletah,* a biblical term that means the *Surviving Remnant*. Samuel Norich, General Manager of the Forward Association who was born in the Feldafing DP camp, addressed the gathering and redefined Sh'erit ha-Pletah as the "Saving" Remnant. I agree. It was not enough to survive, our mission was to save.

That's what Tania Rozmaryn's life has been all about. An educator and volunteer at the U.S. Holocaust Museum, Tania was fifteen years old when she was recruited to teach the orphans at the Bergen Belsen DP camp. She had lost most of the members of her family and it would have been easy to lose her faith.

"But I saw the future," said Tania, "and I knew that if I didn't remain Orthodox I would give Hitler the gift he wanted posthumously." So she made sure her sons received a Jewish education. Today, more than fifty years after Tania made her decision to remain faithful to her Jewishness, she has merited to see her oldest grandchild studying in a Yeshiva in Israel.

The past and the present collided when I attended a panel discussion of the U.S. Army and the DPs. Robert L. Hilliard, a professor of mass communication, talked about the desperate conditions he had witnessed at St. Ottilien when he was a soldier stationed at a nearby air base. After the program, he became elated when I told him I was born there and he informed me of the upcoming international reunion of St. Ottilien alums.

The woman standing next to me, who introduced herself as Yetta Marchuck, said she was also born in the monastery hospital. When she revealed the location of her present address, it turned out to be a small street with only a handful of homes. I know it very well. She lives next door to my Uncle Moishe, the man who saved my mother's life and was therefore ultimately responsible for saving my life and those of my children. The journey that began over a half-century ago continues.

The St. Ottilien Monastery Hospital in 1947.

Helen Zegerman Schwimmer in front of the
St. Ottilien train station in Germany. April 1997.

Devorah and David Zejerman on their wedding day.

1949 Rosha Hashanah Greeting Card.
Devorah, Chaya and David Zejerman.

Devorah Zejerman holding son, Motel, and daughter, Chaya,
in the Gabarzee DP Camp in Munich, Germany. Summer 1950.

Devorah, Chaya, Motel and David Zejerman on the train from their
DP camp in Munich to the port of Bremenhafen, where they will board
the ship bound for United States. January 1951.

The Jews of St. Ottilien

Traditionally, this is the time of year for reunions; however there was nothing traditional about the gathering I attended in West Palm Beach, Florida in May 2000. People who had never met, of different ages and backgrounds, reunited because they shared one common bond, St. Ottilien, a Benedictine Monastery nestled in the idyllic countryside of Upper Bavaria in Germany.

Named for a pious and charitable nun, known as the "saint of vision" because of her remarkable healing powers, the monastery had been converted to a Displaced Persons Camp after the war. It was here that I was born in 1947 when my parents, Polish Jews, were waiting to immigrate to America.

In 1997, I traveled back to Germany to confront my past and to make peace with it. And although I toured the grounds of the monastery and interviewed the monks, it was not until three years later that many of my questions, both personal and historical, would finally be answered by Dr. Robert L. Hilliard. Fate brought us together at a conference on Displaced Persons, sponsored by the Holocaust Museum in Washington, D.C. During a panel discussion on the role of the military in the DP camp experience, I learned of his book, *Surviving The Americans: The Continued Struggle of the Jews After Liberation,* and the miraculous story of the role he played in the lives of the Jews of St. Ottilien.

The Power Of The Pen
In 1945, 19 year-old Robert Hilliard and 25 year-old Edward

Herman, two GIs stationed on an army base in Germany after WW II, were so distressed by the conditions they observed at nearby St. Ottilien they started a massive letter writing campaign to the American people. Ultimately, the contents of the letter came to the attention of President Truman and played a key role in reversing US policy towards the Jews. An excerpt from their lengthy letter, which appears in Dr. Hilliard's book and details the plight of the survivors, reads:

> *At the hospital of St. Ottilien there are today 750 people including a staff of doctors. . .attempting to preserve the life they find it hard to believe they still have. Four months ago this same hospital was being used to care for German soldiers. At the same time there were thousands of Jews roaming Germany, sick, tortured, wounded, without food, clothing or help of any kind. One particular group was led by Dr. Zalman Grinberg. For months he has tried to obtain aid for these people. The Germans refused him. The local governments refused him. . .For these people the Red Cross, UNRRA, the various Hebrew organizations were, although present, nonexistent. If they are to survive the coming winter they need shoes. . .they need sheets and blankets. . .medical supplies. . .the necessities of life and they are depending on you to get it for them. The intolerable situation of the Jews having to beg the Germans for food exists...We are writing to you for you are the only ones that can help. . .These surviving Jews of Europe want to live. The fact that five children have already been born at St. Ottilien is proof enough."*

Olga Salitan was one of those first babies to be born in St. Ottilien. I met her recently during the gathering organized and sponsored by E. Edward Herman, now a retired financier in Palm Beach, and Robert Hilliard, presently a Professor of Mass Communication at Emerson College in Boston. By the time I was born in 1947, conditions at St. Ottilien had greatly improved due to the crusading efforts of these two remarkable men.

"Most of us have no family so when we get together with

survivors we consider them family. That's what our meeting is all about. . .the living," said Jean Einstein, Olga's mother. This same sentiment was echoed by the participants who came from California, Ohio, Wisconsin, Massachusetts, Chicago and New York to join those now residing in Florida.

When I traveled to St. Ottilien three years earlier, I had never met anyone connected with that DP camp. Now, suddenly, I was surrounded by an entirely new "family." The reunion brought together eight St. Ottilien "babies" who were thrilled to have the opportunity to meet each other and Dr. Isaac Vidor, the obstetrician who delivered many of those born in the monastery. The group also consisted of former patients and orphans who brought along family members to share the experience.

My daughter, Sara, accompanied me to Florida and spent the next four days learning first-hand about the DP era as she listened to survivor's stories, looked at the precious photograph albums we each brought along and participated in activities which included a special *Yom Hashoah* (Day of Remembrance of the Holocaust) program at the Holocaust Memorial in Miami Beach; a visit to Florida Atlantic University where we listened to a performance of their klezmer band and viewed the Jewish Library and exceptional work of the Jewish book bindery; a meeting with a member of the Jewish Claims Commission who focused on the status of current negotiations; and discussions about how to locate missing relatives with representatives of the American Red Cross Holocaust and War Victims Tracing and Information Center.

Connecting Past And Present

But it was the conversations with the other survivors, over meals and during the lengthy bus rides that proved to be the most significant part of our reunion. As we got to know each other and caught up on the last 50 plus years, each of us made new connections and discovered old ones.

Philip Sal, who met and married his wife, Esther, in St. Ottilien, had been the ambulance driver who brought patients from Munich to the hospital between 1945-50. More than likely he was the one who had transported my ailing mother from the Gabarze

DP camp to the monastery where she gave birth to me. Yetta Marchuck, who came with her father, Max Goldsammler, was born the same year as I was. Today she lives in a house right next door to my uncle Moshe Berger, my mother's only surviving family member.

Like a pebble thrown into the water that creates ripples far beyond what the eye can see, the two young GIs had poured out their hearts in a letter to the American people that continues to make waves fifty-five years later. As we gathered together on the last evening of our reunion, we presented Bob and Ed with a memento, a photo-poster of the St. Ottilien hospital expressing our gratitude and appreciation for their efforts, then and now and signed by the survivors, their children and their children's children.

Epilogue:

*Robert Hillard's book about the successful campaign he and Ed Herman waged on behalf of the DPs was ultimately made into the award-winning documentary, **Displaced: Miracle at St. Ottilien,** written, directed and produced by John Michalczyk, a former Jesuit priest who is Chair of the Fine Arts Department and Film Studies Program at Boston College.*

*Ed Herman and John Michalczyk again collaborated in 2007 to produce **Creating Harmony**, a film about the St. Ottilien DP Camp Orchestra, based on the book, **Symphony on Fire,** by Sonia Beker, whose parents were musicians who met in the camp. The film presents the life-affirming stories of those survivors who are an example of the resilient, courageous and determined nation that not only rose like a phoenix out of the ashes, but learned to play an inspiring new song.*

I Did Not Forget You

A garden grows in Brooklyn. It has been planted in memory of those who perished and in tribute to those who survived the Holocaust. And blossoming among the trees and shrubs and flowers you will also find these words. . . Kristallnacht . . . Sobibor. . .Emmanuel Ringelblum. . .Ninth Fort. . .Roza Robota . . .Struma. . .Wannsee. . .Hannah Szenes. . .Warsaw Ghetto. . .the vocabulary of the Holocaust, words that instantly recall the terror and the triumph, the hope and the horror.

The heels are tapping, where to, where to, what in?
From the old Vilna streets, they ship us to Berlin.
I need not ask whose, but my heart is rent.
Oh tell me shoe the truth, where were the feet sent?
The feet of those boots, with buttons like dew.
The child of those slippers, the woman of that shoe.
And children's shoes everywhere, why don't I see a child?
Why are the bridal shoes there, not worn by the bride?
Among the children's worn out boots, my mother's shoes
    so fair!
Sabbath was the only day, she donned this footwear.

In these sorrowful words of Abraham Sutzkever from the Vilna Ghetto, we share his grief upon seeing a trainload of shoes, once the property of murdered Jews, being sent to the Germans in Berlin. The words speak to us today from a stone marker in

The Holocaust Memorial Park, located at Shore Boulevard and Emmons Avenue at the foot of Sheepshead Bay, the first outdoor memorial to the victims of the Holocaust in New York City.

As I look out on the ships sitting peacefully in the calm waters of Sheepshead Bay I see another ship, the *Struma*. It is December, 1941 and 769 Jews seeking asylum, board the old 56-foot cattle boat in Constanza, Romania en route to Palestine, where they hope to enter by way of Istanbul. Denied entry by the Turks, who refuse to place them in a transit camp until their journey can be resumed, the passengers are confined to the *Struma* for ten weeks. The British High Commissioner refuses to grant them immigration visas to continue their trip and so the Turkish police tow the *Struma* out to sea, though it carries no food or water or fuel. Within a few hours, the boat is mistakenly torpedoed by a Soviet ship and sinks.

One man, David Stollor, survives to tell the story. It is a story I read for the first time from a stone marker. The memorial site is comprised of 40 such historical markers describing the Holocaust, 24 symbolic markers and 104 additional markers that have been reserved for the names of those that perished.

Another stone reveals the almost prescient words of Dwight D. Eisenhower, Commander of the Allied Forces in Europe, after entering Buchenwald in 1945, words etched in stone that are chilling in light of today's revisionist agenda.

"I have never felt able to describe my emotional reaction when I first came face to face with indisputable evidence of Nazi brutality and ruthless disregard of every shred of decency. I visited every nook and cranny of the camp because I felt it my duty to be in a position from then on to testify first hand about these things in case there ever grew up at home the belief or assumption that these stories of Nazi brutality were just propaganda. I not only did so but as soon as I returned I sent communications to both Washington and London urging the two governments to send instantly to Germany a random group of newspaper editors and representative groups from the national legislature. I felt that the evidence should be

*immediately placed before the American and British publics
in a fashion that would leave no room for cynical doubt."*

Remembrance and Renewal

This park contains both "a memorial that allows us to
remember and the garden to symbolize the renewal of life,"
Brooklyn Borough President Howard Golden announced at the
official dedication ceremony of the **Holocaust Memorial Park** in
1997. He went on to point out that Brooklyn, the borough with
the largest number of survivors and their loved ones, finally has a
gathering place where they could come and pay tribute to the
millions who perished.

Mayor Rudolph Giuliani, speaking directly to the survivors
in the audience, said that "this was a place where we can come to
deal with the tragedy and the triumph of the Jewish people."

Keynote Speaker Abraham Foxman, National Director,
Anti-Defamation League, declared that it has become clear that
whenever people dared to say, "NO!" Jews lived, as he revealed
that his presence at this dedication was made possible by the Gentile
who hid him as a child and saved his life.

"*Mir zinen du se gedenke*n (we are here to remember),"
intoned Pauline Bilus, co-chair with Betty Baranoff of the Holocaust
Memorial Committee. She continued in Yiddish, a language once
marked for annihilation that lives triumphantly on along with the
survivors.

In the distance I can hear the rumble of the elevated train
as I carefully walk along the path where the stone witnesses beckon
to me to listen to their stories. *Sobibor,* a name that's painfully
familiar. Suddenly, I hear the echo of other trains, the ones that
carried the Jews of the Lublin district of Poland to this infamous
death camp. Over 200,000 Jews were murdered in *Sobibor,* among
them Minna, the grandmother I never knew, and her young
children, Ruchel and Sheva and Sara and Ephraim, the aunts and
uncle I never met.

The stone marker engraved with the poignant words of
Simon Wiesenthal, survivor and pursuer of Nazi criminals, is a
fitting acknowledgment of the visionaries who have created this

outdoor museum as a place for reflection and education.

> *"I believe in God and the world to come. When each of us comes before the six million we will be asked what we did with our lives. One will say he became a watchmaker and another will say that he became a tailor. But I will be able to say I did not forget you."*

L'Chaim

I am in Atlanta, Georgia, attending the wedding that was not supposed to be. Seated in the elegant ballroom of the Swiss Hotel, I listen as my dear friend, Debbie, the mother of the bride, offers a toast to the newlyweds.

> "This year, my son and I went with the **March of the Living** to Poland and Israel. From Auschwitz to Treblinka and Majdonik we witnessed destroyed communities that exist only in cemeteries, pits and memories. My parents were not supposed to be, their children and their grandchildren were not supposed to be. The sustaining breath during the March was Shana and David's wedding, a simcha that was also not supposed to be. I am convinced that the punishment for Hitler and his minions is to be the silent guests at every simcha that they had hoped to exterminate. On Friday my father said kaddish because he had yahrzeit for his mother who perished at Sobibor. On Shabbos my father had an aliyah when David HaCohen was called to the Torah for his aufruf, and today my father stood under his granddaughter's chupah and recited one of the sheva brochos. All these were not supposed to be, to be wiped out from existence. And here we are today, living, being, celebrating and very much alive. L'Chaim!"

Debbie's mother was a child of fourteen when she found refuge with a Polish family. Because they hid her in their home, she survived the holocaust, married and today she and her husband are blessed with four children and six grandchildren, a large and loving family that have all gathered together to celebrate this *simcha*.

It is one week later and I'm attending a different kind of simcha. Survivors, their children and their grandchildren have gathered at the **Holocaust Memorial Park** at the foot of Sheepshead Bay in Brooklyn, New York, to honor the memory of Chiune Sugihara. Once again I am reminded that there were righteous Gentiles whose courageous actions would ultimately affect the lives of generations of Jews.

The NYC Commissioner of Consumer Affairs, Jules Polonetsky, introduces his father-in-law, Nathan Lewin, a prominent Washington attorney. When Mr. Lewin was a three-year old child in Lithuania, Chiune Sugihara, the Japanese Consul in Kovno, was faced with a difficult moral dilemma. Should he follow the dictates of his conscience or the orders of his government? His decision to "choose life" made it possible for Nathan Lewin to be standing here today with his wife, his daughter and his son-in-law.

"I'm here to tell you a personal story and deliver a tribute that can never be said often enough," said Mr. Lewin. "Words can kill and words can save and we are here to commemorate a document that saved thousands," he said holding up the visa that saved his own family's life. The details of this incredible rescue effort are simple enough. By 1940 Kovno, Lithuania had become an increasingly dangerous place and the Jews had come up with a plan to leave. Their destination was the Dutch West Indies, which did not require formal entrance visas, but to get there they needed to travel through the Soviet Union via the Trans-Siberian railroad and then by boat to Kobe, Japan.

Although Chiune Sugihara had been appointed to the consulate in Turkey, the Japanese government decided at the very last minute to send him instead to Lithuania. Because this brilliant diplomat was fluent in German and Russian as well as English, French and Chinese, his presence at this geographical crossroads was invaluable. It was also at this time that the Dutch government recalled their pro-Nazi ambassador and appointed businessman Jan Zwartendijk as temporary consul in Kovno.

The stage had been set. Destiny brought these two men together to a place where their actions would have a profound effect on the course of Jewish history. When Jan Zwartendijk agreed to stamp their passports with a Dutch visa to the Caribbean, the Jews then asked Sugihara to issue them Japanese transit visas so they could travel through the Soviet Union and Japan to get to Curacao. Sugihara wired his government three times for permission to provide the Jews with the Japanese visas. Each time he was denied. In defiance of his government he chose to issue the visas saying, "I may have to disobey my government, but if I don't I will be disobeying God."

Hiroki Sugihara was only a little boy but he remembers the torment his father endured when he was unceremoniously dismissed from the foreign ministry because of his decision to help the Jews of Kovno. For one month Chiune Sugihara sat and hand wrote visas which directly saved 6,000 men women and children. However, in these 58 years the number has swelled to 50,000.

"I cannot help but feel my father's presence among us," said Hiroki Sugihara as he accepted the **1997 Holocaust Humanitarian Award** on behalf of his father who passed away in 1986. Hiroki has written an important and moving book called *Visas For Life* about his parents, Chiune and Yukiko, and the significant role they played during this period in our history.

Among the thousands who received those lifesaving visas were the members of the *Mir Yeshiva*, among them Rabbi Moshe Zupnik, Rabbi Chaim Portnoy and Rabbi Jacob Ederman who were young students at the time. Almost sixty years later, they have come to the **Holocaust Memorial Park** to honor Chiune Sugihara.

Attendees were eager to share their stories. Shlomo Fish was a young child when he traveled directly from Berlin to Shanghai with his parents. However, his brother-in-law, Rabbi Aaron Bokow, was one of the students at the Mir Yeshiva who received a passport from Chiune Sugihara. Because the elderly Rabbi Bokow, who is Rabbi Emeritus of the Seabreeze Jewish Center, was unable to attend, Mr. Fish came as his representative. Chaja Haas, another survivor, was only eleven years old when she left Kovno with a Sugihara passport. She too came to express her gratitude.

Rivka, a lovely young teacher, showed me the contents of a small brown cardboard box that is the legacy from her father, Avrum Jodlo. When he was a child in Mezrich, his parents recognized that he was an exceptional student and sent him to study in Kovno. "This is a picture of my father at his Bar Mitzvah." said Rivka. "Here are the letters he received from his parents while he was in the yeshiva." These precious scraps of paper were the only memories her father had left of the family that perished. But it was Chiune Sugihara who provided Avrum Jodlo with the one piece of paper that saved his life, a Japanese visa.

"Whoever sheltered or even simply assisted a Jew risked terrifying punishment. In this regard it is only right to remember that a few thousand Jews survived through the entire Hitlerian period hidden in Germany and Poland in convents, cellars and attics by citizens who were courageous, compassionate and above all sufficiently intelligent to observe for years the strictest discretion."

Primo Levi, *Drowned and The Saved*, 1988.

These words are engraved on one of the 40 historical stone markers in the **Holocaust Memorial Park.** In the year since it opened, the Park has become a meaningful destination for me personally. Whenever I stroll around the beautifully landscaped grounds, enjoying the tranquil setting of the garden, I am drawn once again to the stone marker entitled **"Sobibor."** My friend, Debbie's father, and my mother grew up together in the town of Uchanie. Members of both of our families died in Sobibor, the death camp where the Jews of the Lublin district of Poland were exterminated. As I bear witness before the sanctified granite stone, it is a poignant reminder that I am the daughter that was not supposed to be. *L'Chaim.*

Miracle At Kovno

There are miracles that announce their presence with the force of lightning. Others go about their work quietly, without fanfare, so that the full impact of their power may not be recognized for many years to come. This is the story of just such a miracle, a signature on a piece of paper that affected the lives of generations and ultimately influenced the course of history.

It is the summer of 1940 and Lithuania has been annexed by the Soviet Union. Jan Zwartendijk, a Dutch businessman who represents the Phillips Electronics Corporation in the region, is appointed temporary Dutch Consul in Kovno after Holland recalls its ambassador upon learning he's a Nazi sympathizer. Fearful for the fate of observant Jews under the new communist regime, two Dutch citizens studying at the Telshe Yeshiva in Vilna ask Zwartendijk to help them escape to Curacao in the Dutch West Indies. It is at this point that the story begins to take on heroic dimensions.

Jan Zwartendijk could have easily turned his back on the students' plights. However, despite the risk of retribution from the Nazis upon his return to Holland, Zwartendijk provided the young men with papers and then deliberately exceeded his authority by issuing a total of 1,200 fraudulent Curacao visas! Many were used by entire families and others were reused several times after they were sent back to friends and relatives in Vilna.

Armed with these pieces of paper, Jews were then able to obtain transit visas from Japanese diplomat Chiune Sugihara enabling over 2200 refugees to escape to Shanghai via the trans-Siberian railroad. These included the intellectual elite, outstanding rabbis, Talmudic scholars and the entire faculty and students of the Mirrer Yeshiva, the only Yeshiva saved intact from the Holocaust. Many of those rescued by Zwartendijk went on to found leading Jewish educational institutions, thereby reviving a Jewish people that was on the brink of extinction.

Renaissance of Judaism

"This entire group was to have a profound impact on the postwar renaissance of Judaism throughout the world," according to Dr. David Kranzler, the noted Holocaust scholar and historian. The compelling story of Jan Zwartendijk, the "Angel of Mercy" is revealed in Dr. Kranzler's landmark text, *Japanese, Nazis and Jews: The Jewish Refugee Community of Shanghai, 1938-1945.*

Jan Zwartendijk, who died in 1976, is an example of that "rare individual who can achieve immortality in but one moment," suggested Dr. Kranzler. During his lifetime, he sought neither recognition nor honor for his actions which he did out of a simple sense of decency.

Fifty-six years after the miracle at Kovno, the Jewish people welcomed the opportunity to finally show their gratitude. On May 16, 1996 Jan Zwartendijk was honored posthumously at Boys' Town in Bayit Vegan, Jerusalem in the presence of his sons, Jan and Robert, his daughter, Edith Fes, Dutch, Israeli and American dignitaries and many of the survivors he saved.

Tears From Heaven

"One of the foundations of Judaism is expressing gratitude," explained Rabbi Moshe Linchner, the founder of Boys' Town, who studied with rabbis saved by Zwartendijk. "There is no more appropriate place than here, at the gates of Jerusalem, to show our gratitude to this messenger of G-d who saved the Torah for the Jewish people." In a moving ceremony, Boys' Town dedicated the Jan Zwartendijk Memorial Garden and established the Jan Zwartendijk Perpetual Scholarship Endowment.

Because Boys' Town has provided a home and educational

facilities for orphans from the Holocaust and underprivileged boys from all over the world since 1948, "it is a very appropriate place to memorialize my father," said Robert Zwartendijk. "I was most impressed by the values you teach your students here." Dr. Jan Zwartendijk noted, "This year would have been my father's 100th birthday. You couldn't have given him a more appropriate present than a scholarship at this school in his memory."

A Dutch Holocaust survivor, whose sons had studied at Boys' Town, paid tribute to the Zwartendijk family by recounting her experiences. "A Jew wanted to go to only one destination in those days," Lea DeLange told a hushed gathering. "A shelter, a political refuge, it does not matter where, in Antarctica or on the equator, a shelter. And Jan Zwartendijk opened a door to such a shelter on a small island called Curacao, an island in the Dutch realm. In so doing he tied his name to our nation forever. A noble man, an innocent and honest man called Jan Zwartendjik. Don't forget."

During the dedication ceremony, it suddenly began to rain, which is unusual for Israel at this time of year. Rabbi Gray cited Jewish sources that say that G-d cries when the righteous die and suggested the rain was "tears from heaven in memory of this great man." Dr. Kranzler revealed that efforts are underway to have the heroic deeds of this Righteous Gentile recognized by Yad Vashem.

Rescue and Reflection

Upon his return to the United States, Dr. Jan Zwartendijk reflected on his trip to Israel and spoke passionately about the impact of his experiences there. "More than half a century after my father's brief consular career, I was stunned by the tremendous outpouring of gratitude to him at several occasions during our visit to Jerusalem," he said. "The memorable tribute was even more remarkable as Boys' Town, through Rabbi Gray in New York, had only learned in recent months from Dr. Kranzler about my father's largely unrecognized deeds. Boys' Town deserves the highest praise for the imaginative and energetic way in which it reacted to hearing of my father's role in the mass escape of Polish Jews from Lithuania."

During their stay in Jerusalem, Dr. Kranzler had arranged for the family to visit the *Mirrer Yeshiva* where the survivors who had escaped Lithuania with the help of the Curacao visas were eager to recount the details of their rescue. "Two vivid impressions stand out," Dr. Zwartendijk recalled. "The first is the realization that my father's actions have rippled outward over the last half century to touch the lives not only of those he helped save, but of their children and grandchildren. It is a touching thought that his deeds may serve as an example, perhaps even an inspiration, to the young men at Boys Town and others."

"Second," he continued. "I was overwhelmed to actually talk with some of the survivors. It is one thing to know on paper that many people escaped. It is quite another to shake the hand of a person pouring out gratitude to your father for his very life."

Under the patronage of the Dutch and Israeli governments, Boys' Town Jerusalem will honor Jan Zwartendijk at its international Dinner of Tribute. According to Michael Scharf, President of Boys' Town Jerusalem, the school is honoring him "as a long overdue token of gratitude because much of the Jewish moral heritage taught at the school today was preserved and passed along by the Jews he saved."

The Heroes Among Us

They live among us, quietly going about their ordinary lives. They shop alongside us in the supermarket. They sit beside us on buses and trains, traveling at half fare like all the other senior citizens. But these are no ordinary citizens. Look beyond the gray, thinning hair, the wrinkled skin and the slightly stooped gait and you will discover you are in the presence of a hero, a fearless fighter who once took on the most evil empire imaginable and won.

And on a perfect spring afternoon in Brooklyn, New York, the heroic deeds of these members of an elite fighting brigade known as the *Bielski Partisans* were finally being publicly recognized and commemorated.

"This is the 17th year of the Holocaust Memorial Gathering and I have never been moved to tears like this," said Ira Bilus, member of the Presidium of the Holocaust Memorial Committee as he read from the Oxford University Press book, **Defiance: The Bielski Partisans.** The author, Nechama Tec, Professor of Sociology at University of Connecticut, Stamford, sat in the front row and listened as Bilus described Tuvia Bielski, the charismatic leader who became know as Yehudah HaMaccabee.

A granite marker in the Holocaust Memorial Park briefly details the history of the Bielski partisans. After their parents and other family members were killed by the Germans when they invaded the family's village near Novogrudok, the three Bielski brothers fled to the forests. Tuvia, who had been a Polish corporal before the war, was chosen as the commander of a small group of partisans composed of the Jews remaining in the region's ghettos.

The Bielski brigade operated from deep within the Naliboki Forest, avenging the murder of Jews by Belorussia police and local farmers. From a small band of 30 men, the group ultimately numbered 1,250 men, women and children. This was the largest Jewish partisan group during the Holocaust and their fortification boasted a hospital with doctors and nurses, as well as blacksmiths, bakers, a school and a synagogue.

Robert Bielski, joined by his mother Lillian, accepted the 2001 Holocaust Humanitarian Award honoring his late father, which was presented by Pauline Bilus, Director of the Holocaust Memorial Committee. "There isn't a person sitting here today who has not been touched personally by a madman seeking to annihilate our people, but we are the survivors," the hero's son announced. He pointed out that over 10,000 Jews are descendants from the original group of partisans, testament to one of the bravest inspiring acts of our history. "The Bielskis took Jews out of the grasp of Nazis and certain death and brought them to the forests. This was the largest armed rescue of Jews by Jews."

As Robert Bielski called out the names of the children and grandchildren of the Bielski brothers, they ascended the stage and he proudly proclaimed, "These are the survivors, these are the miracles." And with a voice filled with emotion he revealed that Miramax Films recently bought the rights to the story and would bring the heroic saga to the screen.

"The Bielskis never bent a knee, never bowed, never wore a yellow star," he continued. Together the brothers commanded the group like a military machine. It was a shtetel and they called it "Yerushalayim." Among the over 1,250 Jews whose lives were saved were Sol and Ruth Lapidus, Frieda and Joe Feit, and Lea and Abie Kutler, all present at the gathering, who stood up to resounding applause.

As a member of the second generation, I always found it regrettable that the Jews who defied the Nazi regime's death sentence were labeled survivors and generally portrayed as hapless victims who managed to survive by some fortuitous circumstances.

I know how hard my mother, father and uncle fought to prevent their annihilation. But the reality is that everyone who defied Hitler's decree was a hero by virtue of their determination to live. These men, women and children did not merely survive. They chose life.

When my daughter, Sara, and I were given the honor of lighting one of the six memorial candles in commemoration of those who perished, I recalled the moving invocation by Rabbbi Joseph Singer, Rabbi Emeritus, Manhattan Beach Jewish Center. "In this park we find tombstones without graves. In Europe we have bodies and ashes without tombstones. The meaning of dedication is to unite ourselves with the souls of those not buried who are hovering everywhere."

Into the Arms of Strangers:
A Daughter's Tribute

It began with the discovery of a stack of letters written to Sylva Avramovici by her parents. Treasured remnants of a lost childhood, the letters had been hidden away for over half a century. "My dearest little mouse," each letter from Sylva's father Avram began. "Be a very good little girl," he gently advised his eleven year-old daughter, his only child, whom he had sent away to freedom. "Be obedient."

When conditions in Germany grew more ominous following Kristalnacht, concerned and influential British Jews proposed a life-saving plan to their government. Permit the temporary admission of young children and teenagers whose lives were in peril and the Jewish community would finance the operation to ensure that none of the refugees became a burden on the public.

A similar plan had come before the U.S. Congress, but was defeated by the powerful anti-immigration lobby. However, the British House of Commons accepted the initiative, and the mechanism for selecting, processing and transporting the children began. The first train left Berlin on December 1, 1938. The "kindertransport," as the miraculous rescue mission came to be called, placed thousands of children in foster homes throughout England between 1938 and 1939 with the intention of reuniting them with their parents after the war. However, the majority of the children, including little Sylva Avramovici, never saw their parents again.

Tracing Her Roots

Deborah Oppenheimer grew up on Long Island aware that her mother had been one of the children rescued by the *"kindertransport."* But she knew nothing of her mother's interrupted childhood or the tragic details of her wartime experiences, a topic that was always too painful for her mother to discuss. And so the past eluded Deborah until her father found the secret cache of letters after her mother's death. They were lovingly written each day by her grandparents in Germany and sent to her mother in England. Crossing a continent and an ocean, the fragile little pieces of paper reached their destination, miraculously surviving the destruction taking place around them.

Deborah describes the discovery of the letters as *bashert*. It's a word that comes up frequently in conversation with this sensitive and talented woman who is now a successful Hollywood producer. Upon graduating from the University of New York at Buffalo, she got involved in television as a "fluke" and began her career working on programs for HBO under Gerald Levin. After reading her grandparents' letters, Deborah was determined to share this riveting story of heroism with a world that had become familiar with the gruesome details of the Holocaust but had never heard of the extraordinary rescue mission known as the *"kindertransport."*

"It was astonishing to hold the letters in my hands," Deborah recalls. "They made my grandparents come alive for the first time. It was so startling to realize that my mother was a child who had been deeply, deeply loved by her parents," she continued. "That was the first of the endless discoveries in the process of making this film which has been filled with amazing revelations." The courage and resolve it must have taken for parents to make the painful decision to send away their children further fueled Deborah's own resolve to tell this story of unparalleled love and sacrifice.

And so began her three year journey into the past which covered thousands of miles researching the people and places that had been crucial to the success of the rescue mission. After traveling to her mother's birthplace in Chemnitz, Germany, she visited several concentration camps, including Auschwitz/Birkenau and

Theresienstadt, as well as Jewish communities in Prague, Budapest and Berlin. Deborah Oppenheimer could never have predicted when she began working on this project how the experience would forever change her life.

The *Kinder's* Legacy

Once again, the benevolent hand of fate intervened. Gerald Levin had now become the Chairman of Time-Warner and when Deborah approached her former boss with the idea for the documentary he gave the project his blessing. "I received support from the highest levels," said Deborah, who is especially grateful to Barry Meyer who gave the go-ahead to Warner Brothers to make the film. "I believe the entire project was *bashert*."

Deborah assembled an award winning team for this labor of love that ultimately became a powerful and inspiring new film, *Into The Arms of Strangers: Stories of the Kindertransport.* The film is narrated by Oscar winner, Dame Judy Dench, who experienced the bombing of London as a child during the war and was honored to be involved with the project. *Into The Arms of Strangers* is directed by Mark Jonathan Harris, writer and director of the Academy Award-Winning *The Long Way Home*, with a musical score composed by Emmy Award winner Lee Holdridge. The filmmakers also unearthed rarely-seen archival footage depicting haunting scenes of a world that now exists only in the memories of the survivors.

The U.S. Holocaust Museum, the Simon Wiesenthal Center, newspaper articles, fortuitous encounters and the discovery of a Kindertransport Association provided invaluable information, leading Deborah to surviving *kinder*, most of whom were now in their seventies. The clock was ticking and so the team had to work quickly, interviewing these *kinder* who were scattered all over the globe, including New Zealand, Israel and England. According to Deborah, the adult *kinder* were eager to do the interviews "to preserve their story, to honor their parents and as a legacy to their children and grandchildren."

Each of the sixteen "kinder" who appear in the film provides the audience with vivid and poignant descriptions of their parents, their rescuers and their lives, which at times took heroic turns. Jack Hellman and a group of 26 children were brought to England by Baron James de Rothschild. Worried about the fate of his family, Jack relates how he innocently approached Baron Rothschild at his stately mansion, asking him for a work permit for his father. The Baron was so impressed by the child's courage he agreed, and as a result Jack's parents arrived in England on the day before Hitler invaded Poland.

Alexander Gordon was one of the first to leave Germany on the kindertransport. However, once the war began he was considered an enemy alien by the British government because he was now over sixteen. In heartbreaking detail he describes how he was arrested and shipped off to prison in Australia for a year until he volunteered to join the Pioneer Corps and was brought back to England to fight in the war.

Rescuer Norbert Wollheim was a twenty-five year old social worker when he began organizing the kinder transports in Berlin. He negotiated with the Nazis, worked with the British, met the parents and traveled as an escort on the trains saving between six and seven thousand children.

"This is a story of rescue. . .it is about love, loss, survival and memory." said Deborah. "I feel grateful to have been involved in telling the remarkable story of the *kindertransport* because it has touched so many people who have found it uplifting and hopeful."

The project originally began as a way for Deborah Oppenheimer to deal with her own personal grief over the death of her mother. In the process she succeeded in creating a loving tribute to all of the devoted Jewish mothers and fathers who made the ultimate sacrifice when they sent their kinder "Into the Arms of Strangers."

Epilogue:

In the year 2000 **Into the Arms of Strangers** received the *Academy Award for Best Documentary Feature Film.*

In Tune With the Melody of Life

Blackjack!" Rose Friedman answered enthusiastically when I asked how many grandchildren she had. She was not boasting, just grateful that the gamble she took almost fifty years ago paid off beyond her wildest dreams. After surviving death marches, concentration camps and a life-threatening illness, she emigrated to America, where she found herself confronted with a different kind of challenge.

"You'll never get married," friends warned her when she refused to date on Shabbos.

"So I won't get married," recalls the feisty grandmother of twenty-one. "Everyone told me that in America, if a boy asks you out on Saturday you'd better go." But while all her friends rushed to embrace a secular lifestyle and urged her to do the same, Rose continued to have faith in herself and in G-d. It was this determination that helped save her life when everyone around her was dying.

"We were four girls and our job was to carry the bodies out of the barracks. By the time the Americans liberated us from Bergen Belsen, the other three were dead and I was dying from typhus," said Rose describing the nightmare that engulfed her. The Red Cross transferred her to a hospital in Sweden where she was finally cured and then her uncle brought her to America. While her only surviving sister married a man who was not religious, Rose refused to compromise. She met her match in night school.

Rosie Farkas of Prague married Yitzak Friedman of

Studanow, Czechoslovakia, forty-nine years ago in the Bronx. Although there are no photographs of their wedding, the day is permanently etched in her memory. "My aunt made sandwiches, cold cuts," Rose recalls fondly, "and a man played the fiddle." For this bride the only tunes that sound sweeter than those played at her wedding are the holy melodies sung by her husband.

"G-d Watched Over Me"

By the time he was fourteen, Yitzak's musical gift was already apparent, so in spite of his age the rabbis permitted him to sing *chazzunus*, because his davening gave everyone such pleasure. He was the youngest of seven children who grew up in the warm and loving community of the Satmar Chasidim. But the singing suddenly stopped when Yitzak was nineteen. The war forced him to leave his idyllic life on the farm and become a soldier in the Czech army and then an officer in the Hungarian army. By 1944 Yitzak's world was reduced to the deadly landscape of the Holocaust, as he was shuffled from Auschwitz to Birkenau to Maulthausen and finally Abenzay. He survived, he is convinced, "only because G-d watched over me."

After the liberation, while he was stranded in Italy for five years waiting to emigrate to America, he learned the tragic details about his family. Two brothers were killed in the army. A third was killed in hiding. His father and two sisters perished in the camps. But the most painful news involved the fate of another sister and his mother who were hidden by a Polish family in Galicia. Miraculously, they survived the war, but one day as she was out looking for food, two Ukrainians caught his sister and when she innocently led them back to her mother, they killed both of them.

Many survivors were so devastated by the loss of their families that they also lost their faith. "I grew up with a Chasid who attended the Lubliner Yeshiva" Yitzak recalls sadly. "When I met him after the war, his beard and payess were gone and he no longer kept kosher or Shabbos. G-d, he told me, didn't like him and had taken away his wife and children, so maybe G-d would like him better now."

He goes on to relate the story of a man who sought out a

learned rabbi and asked him, "Who do you give the biggest *koved* (respect), a rav who is a scholar or a rebbe who is descended from rebbeim?"

The sage answered. "Not a rav and not a rebbe. The biggest respect goes to the man who survived the Holocaust and still wears a yarmulke on his head."

And so in spite of the unbelievable acts of torture and murder that Yitzak witnessed he continued "to declare the praise of Hashem." On the second day after arriving in New York, Yitzak, who was now known as Jack, found a job as a spotter removing stains from silk. His boss, who was Jewish and knew that Jack was observant, insisted he continue to work until 5 o'clock on Friday, even when the days got shorter. His response? "I survived Hitler and I'll overcome you, too, I told him and I quit."

His next job lasted twenty-five years. He worked for the Balnor Corporation, which made plastic swimming pools, and he became the supervisor and then the foreman of the factory. That was his day job. Asked to lead the davening one Friday night in a local shul, the congregation was so impressed with his ability that he was hired for the second day of Passover in a synagogue that held over 1800. His career as a chazzan had begun.

"Come Before Him With Joyous Song"

As his reputation grew, so did the demand for his singing and his supporters suggested he meet with Chazzan Levine of Williamsburg. The chazzan, who was a great teacher, told him, "Young man, you need three things to succeed: voice, voice and voice." After listening to Jack Friedman, he was overwhelmed by his vocal abilities. "A voice like yours is very had to find," said the chazzan and he suggested Jack study seriously. "I took a couple of lessons, but I couldn't attend a cantorium because by then I had small children to support."

The cantor, who never had formal training and composed most of his own melodies, retired in 1997 after an illustrious career that has spanned forty-five years. Having recently celebrated his eightieth birthday, Jack Friedman believes that "Experience is the best teacher. Emotion cannot be taught." For the past thirty years he has served as the chazzan of the Hebrew Alliance in Brooklyn, New York, where the publisher of the *Jewish Press*, Rabbi Sholom Klass, was an ardent admirer. And for thirteen years Cantor Friedman also conducted the Rosh Chodesh services at the Seabreeze Jewish Center.

During a recent visit with one of his children, who lives in Israel, Jack davened in a Chasidic shul. When one of the congregants learned that Jack was a survivor of the Holocaust. he brought his two small sons to services to meet him.

"Reb Yitzak," pleaded the Chasid. "Please bless my children."

"But I'm not a Rebbe," argued the man who spent his life singing G-d's praises.

The younger man responded with tears in his eyes, "You are more than a Rebbe."

What has been the deepest source of inspiration for Jack Friedman? "In dreams my father comes to me and he asks, Yitzak, did you daven today?"

His children, his grandchildren and his great- grandchildren are living proof that the chazzan *ot git gedavened* (had prayed well).

IV

The Philadelphia Story

W hen I met my husband, Richard, he was a freshman at Jefferson Medical College and I was in my senior year at Brooklyn College. After I graduated in 1969 with a degree in English, we were married and began our life together in Philadelphia where he was attending school. My first job, editorial secretary for the Annals of the American Academy of Political and Social Science, was long on title but short on salary and creativity. The only interesting person in that otherwise stuffy enclave was Mary Jane, originally from the heart of Dixie, who had been actively involved in the election of Richard Nixon. We were both intrigued. Where I came from, you didn't meet many charming southern Republicans. And I was her first Brooklyn Jew.

Not only had Mary Jane attended the inauguration, but she had been rewarded for her campaign efforts with several copies of the impressive invitation. When she presented one of these mementos to me I filed it away never suspecting that one day my official invitation to the 1968 Presidential Inauguration would become a prized historical document as a result of Nixon's Watergate "tsuris."

It was at my next job as Continuity Director for Cox & Tanz Advertising, a small full house agency, that I finally had the opportunity to tap into my writing skills. Under the guidance of co-owners, Eugene Tanz and Rita Bilyi, I became a jack-of-all-trades, designing newspaper and magazine ads as well as writing and producing radio and television commercials. I even hired my husband to do the voice over in a radio spot I created for a bank, casting him in the role of a medical student who needed a loan. The gig earned him ten dollars, a windfall which bought us dinner for two and a movie!

When Richard graduated from Jefferson in 1971, he accepted a pediatric internship at Montefiore Hospital in the Bronx. We left Philadelphia and moved back to New York where I went to work for Aladdin Advertising, which placed print ads in several publications including **The Jewish Press.** One year, for our official holiday greeting card, the agency's graphic designer drew each member of the staff making a pithy remark. Incredibly, my line was, "Tell the Jewish Press to hold the back page!" Once again, who could have predicted what the future would hold?

Although it's been over thirty years since we left the city of brotherly love, we still have a great deal of affection for "our first home" and have returned many times to Philadelphia. During one such visit we met world renowned surgeon and cancer researcher, Dr. Judah Folkman, when he was invited to my husband's alma mater to deliver the prestigious Annual Martin E. Rehfuss Lecture. His pioneering exploits had already been the subject of a PBS documentary and a best-selling biography so now it was time for a profile in the **Jewish Press.** When I contacted him in Boston in 2001, he graciously made room in his busy schedule for a revealing, in-depth interview.

Moses Judah Folkman, MD: The Rabbi-Like Doctor

The young child gripped his father's hand tightly as they entered the hospital room together. The boy could see a figure peering grimly out at them from inside the plastic tent that surrounded the bed, but as they moved closer the patient's face brightened and he began to smile broadly. It was the early 1940s when the life-saving treatment for heart attack victims was to envelop them in plastic oxygen tents.

Rabbi Jerome Folkman understood that the presence of a child immediately lifted the spirits of anyone isolated in these tents. If children were allowed into their rooms, patients reasoned, it meant that they weren't that critically ill. And so when his son turned seven he was given the privilege of accompanying his father to minister to hospitalized members of his Reform congregation in Grand Rapids, Michigan. Rabbi Folkman expected that his son, who was descended from nine generations of rabbis, would also become a rabbi.

During these weekend visits, while the child watched and listened to his father talk and pray with the patients and their families, he became aware of another powerful presence in the room. The doctor, the child perceived, was the one who was actually allowed to enter the tent and do things for the patient.

"I think I'll be a doctor," the boy told his father. He thought the news might upset him, but instead, Rabbi Folkman responded prophetically, "Then you'll be a *rabbi-like* doctor."

What's In A Name

A Hebrew name, according to our sages, defines a person's essence and purpose in life.   Moses Judah Folkman, the little boy who aspired to be a doctor, would ultimately fulfill his father's mandate to "be a credit to your people."   But like his rabbinical namesake, Dr. Folkman's forty-year trek through the medical frontier was fraught with obstacles as the surgeon who ventured into the unchartered terrain of cancer laboratory research was labeled a heretic and often ostracized.

While he was Chief of Surgery at Boston Children's Hospital, Dr. Judah Folkman (as he is known professionally) noticed that tumors consisted of thousands of new blood vessels which were visible during surgery but collapsed immediately after the tumor was removed. He theorized that cancer cells have the ability to stimulate the formation of blood vessels which nourish them, a process called *angiogenesis*. Researchers, mainly pathologists who were working with already dead tumor tissue and therefore couldn't see the vessels, ridiculed Dr. Folkman's theory. Although he felt the criticism was incorrect, he knew he couldn't argue the case until he did years of painstaking experiments to support his idea.

"There's a fine line between persistence and obstinacy in research," notes Dr. Folkman, who is currently the Director of the Surgical Research Laboratory at Boston Children's Hospital and Professor of Pediatric Surgery and Professor of Cell Biology at Harvard Medical School.

"If you keep on going year after year and you succeed, people look back and say, oh it was because of the admirable quality of persistence," he says good-naturedly. "But if it doesn't work, then they say you're obstinate, pigheaded, wedded to theory, stiff-necked and rigid. There's a very fine difference and you never know while you're doing it whether you've crossed the line."

It helps to have a sense of humor, he suggests, because the criticism never stops. It took thirty years, but he was finally vindicated when a review by a group of scientists in **Nature Magazine** stated that the hypothesis put forward in 1971 by Folkman has now been confirmed genetically.

Revelation

Dr. Folkman is scrupulous about sharing the spotlight with a variety of colleagues and collaborators. This generosity of spirit is a sign of the deep humility of this modest, unpretentious man. He credits Michael Klagsbrun, who was a member of his laboratory and is now a professor at Harvard, and Yuen Shing, a biochemist, with advancing the first breakthrough in 1983 when they succeeded in purifying the first angiogenic protein. Once their discovery was published in *Science Magazine,* "many critics were converted to competitors," he noted.

According to Dr. Folkman, the most stunning breakthrough came as a result of a paper published in 1989 in *Cell Magazine* by Noel Bouck, a professor at Northwestern University. She proposed that tumors have a balance of stimulators that create blood vessels and inhibitors which discourage their production.

"During the following months I was trying to make a connection with our work," said Dr. Folkman. "Many times you're puzzled and can't figure something out and half the time you never figure it out. However, there have been times when a solution suddenly broke through."

Inspiration comes when you least expect it, but for the rabbi's son revelation came on the holiest day of the year. "It was 10 o'clock in the morning and I can remember precisely where I was sitting and the exact moment during the Yom Kippur service," Dr. Folkman marveled, "when I finally solved the problem that had been puzzling researchers."

Although he must have described the process hundreds of times, his enthusiasm remains unabated. Patiently, Dr. Folkman explains that often when you remove a tumor, a metastasis, a remote site, begins to appear. The metastasis was microscopic and lay dormant, but once you remove the main tumor, you are also removing the source of the inhibitors which have previously swamped the metastasis and prevented its growth. Main tumors can control the remote metastasis by virtue of controlling their angiogenesis, the production of blood vessels feeding the tumor.

This unifying idea led to the discovery by Dr. Michael O'Reilly, in Folkman's lab in 1991, of angiostatin and endostatin, the drugs which inhibit the growth of new blood vessels to tumors. These drugs, which stop cancer by cutting off their blood supply, are now undergoing intensive clinical trials before they can be approved by the FDA and offered as an alternative to the more toxic and less effective chemotherapy, radiation and surgery.

Modern-Day Warrior

For Judah Folkman, the most gratifying aspect of his discovery has been the ability to understand how angiogenesis works not only in tumors, but that it is fundamental to almost every specialty that has diseases that are due to angiogenesis. For example, he points out, the ophthalmologist who is trying to stop blood vessel growth in the eyes so they don't bleed and cause blindness, and the rheumatologist trying to stop blood vessel growth in joints are dealing with the same process. Equally exciting is the flip side where some drugs are being developed to purposely "turn on" angiogenesis to cure diseases of the heart.

Had his sole accomplishment been the pioneering advances in the field of cancer it would have been enough, however, during his productive career Dr. Folkman has participated in the development of an impressive list of life-saving discoveries, beginning at a young age. While he was still an undergraduate at Ohio State University, he was a co-author with Dr. Robert Zollinger on papers describing a new method of removing cancerous parts of the liver.

As a student at Harvard Medical School, he worked in Dr. Robert Gross' lab where he developed the first atrio-ventricular implantable pacemaker, shades of his childhood exposure to heart patients. And during his stint as a lieutenant in the U.S. Navy, stationed at the National Naval Medical Center in Bethesda in 1962, Dr. Folkman and David Long first reported the use of silicone rubber implantable polymers for the sustained-release of drugs, which became the basis for the development of "Norplant." It was here that the seeds for his future research into angiogenesis were also nurtured.

When reviewing the extraordinary career of Dr. Judah Folkman, it's natural to wax biblical. Just as Moses led the ancient

Israelites out of physical and spiritual bondage offering them "a tree of life" to bond to, this modern-day visionary is offering a life-saving alternative to conventional cancer treatments with his discovery of antiangiogenesis therapy. (Even the name has biblical overtones). His groundbreaking contributions have recently been recognized in a PBS Television documentary "Cancer Warrior," as well as an acclaimed biography by science writer Robert Cooke, titled *Dr. Folkman's War.*

When this exceptionally gifted surgeon and researcher, who holds degrees from five universities and is the author of more than 300 peer-reviewed papers, seeks refuge from the language of medicine, he finds it in his wife's voice. Paula Folkman performs professionally year-round with the Tanglewood Symphony Festival Chorus.

"She's a wonderful woman," he says with genuine admiration. It was his sister, Joy, who introduced him to Paula, when the two women were students at Wellesley and he was a surgical resident at Massachusetts General in Boston. Joy is a teacher who is married to world-renowned cardiologist, Dr. Arthur Moss. Another brother, David, is a graduate of Harvard Business School. The Folkmans have two children – Laura, a teacher who recently made them grandparents with the birth of a daughter, and Marjorie, a modern ballet dancer.

Bessie Schomer and Jerome Folkman, descendents of German and Hungarian immigrants, merited seeing their son realize the American dream. A brilliant teacher and compassionate healer, Moses Judah Folkman is a modern-day hero in starched white coat, armed with scalpel and microscope who triumphed over mankind's arch nemesis, cancer. This is the stuff legends are made of.

V

Of Moose and Phish

*A*fter completing his Pediatric residency in 1974, my husband was among the last group of doctors drafted into the military. When we told family and friends that we were going to be stationed at Loring, a remote and isolated Strategic Air Command base located in caribou country in the northern most part of Maine, we were greeted with blank stares.

Public recognition came many years later when the hit sci-fi movie **War Games,** revealed that the site of the first Soviet launched missile attack on the U.S. was our own Loring Air Force Base. Its eventual demise didn't come about as a result of war however, but of peace, when the base was closed for business in 1994 due to the end of the cold war.

Southern Maine's tourist dollars didn't reach that far north, so the closure of the base was a severe blow to the economy of the once thriving potato farming community. News that the town fathers had come up with the brilliant idea of renting the abandoned base to the popular rock band **Phish** was carried by the New York papers when the group gave a history-making summer concert that attracted *over 60,000 people.*

We remember Loring summers that were short, but magical. Our son, Joshua, who had spent the first two years of his life confined to a city apartment now had a backyard and the run of the base as his playground, except for a few restricted areas like the runways where they kept the B-52 bombers.

Winter brought plenty of snow for cross country skiing and snowmobiling. However, average snowfalls which exceeded 110 inches plus the six hour round trip drive from Bangor, the closest Jewish community, prevented their rabbi, who was also our chaplain, from visiting the base very often.

Fast forward twenty-five years. I am interviewing author Rivka Zakutinsky about her latest book, when she casually mentions that when they were newlyweds, her husband Moshe's first position was rabbi, mohel and shochet for the Jewish community of Bangor, Maine. He also served as chaplain to the Jews of Loring Air Force Base.

Ladies Who Lunch

*A*round Sarah's Table is a book about "ladies who lunch." But any resemblance to the *tell-all genre* of contemporary literature ends there because you won't find these women ensconced in a trendy Manhattan locale. Instead, they eagerly gather at the Boro Park home of Sarah Mandel where lunch is the entrée to learn every Tuesday afternoon.

> *"Tuesday is the day that good is doubled, for on the first Tuesday of creation, God himself said twice, 'Behold it is good.' Tuesday is a day to be savored, a day second only to Shabbos in its sweetness and blessing. Tuesday. The day of Sarah's table."*

Enter Sarah's home and you encounter the world of the Hasidic woman. Rivka Zakutinsky and Yaffa Leiba Gottlieb have written a book which introduces us to the long sleeved, high neckline world of *shetels* and *shidduchim*, of modesty and mikvahs, a world few outsiders have been invited to enter until now. But leave your stereotypes at the door as the authors provide an intimate, realistic glimpse into the diverse and complex lives of these modern ultra orthodox women.

For an appetizer we begin with the journey of Susan/Shaina who speaks knowingly to those of us who have gone to the "other side." For Shaina, a children's book author from the Midwest who now calls Crown Heights home, major changes like diet, wardrobe and name, were easy. It was reconciling her new life with the old relationships that proved most difficult, especially with her secular mother, who was mystified when her Susan inexplicably morphed into Shaina, a Hasid who rejected academia for a life of Torah.

And so as the women mine the riches from our heritage, along with a *heimishe* helping of baked salmon, we also savor their insights into the Torah portion of the week. Here is Reva, the publisher, trying to glean a message for her own life from the trials and travails of our ancestors. For Reva middle age has brought the challenge of coping with her husband's illness, "the tyrant that measured out their lives." In this haven created by Sarah she shares her disappointments and her fears with the women who have become her support group. With a touch of humor and a side order of candor, Reva reminisces about her experiences as a new bride and regales the women with her adventures at a makeshift *mikvah*, a secluded lake in Bangor, Maine.

One by one we befriend the Tuesday afternoon regulars. We get to know Klara, the lawyer from Russia; Erica, the stressed-out new stepmother; and Margie, the activist who never sleeps, but keeps a watchful eye on Israel. We meet Glicka, whose life of privilege in Toronto collapsed with the fall of her husband's financial empire. Thanks to Sarah's direction, she is about to discover a new source of enrichment.

Also seated at the table is Tamar, who is preoccupied with the dilemma of helping her daughter find her *bashert*. When it comes to the protocols of matchmaking, these women believe that "children allow parents to pan for gold so they themselves may select the nugget." Sarah's own unconventional meeting with her bashert, the result of a mix-up in plane seats, ultimately received the OK stamp of approval from none other than the Lubavitcher Rebbe.

Did I mention that this is a book of non-fiction based on the lives of the women who actually gather around Sarah's table? Anyone familiar with this community will immediately recognize Sarah, the hostess, the facilitator par excellence.

"Merging the upper and lower worlds by infusing everything with Godliness, a uniquely human task, seemed Sarah's mission. 'Every detail in Sarah's house . . .the hand-painted murals on the walls, these real linen tablecloths, these floral china place settings and glass stemware, that gorgeous chandelier – this is all Sarah's equipment for her personal service to the Creator."

She has had an admirable role model, her mother, the legendary proprietor of an unassuming restaurant on 13th Avenue. Every day, Mrs. Resnick (a nom de plume) personally serves up hearty meals and raises the spirits of those whose hearts have grown heavy.

These are remarkable women who have an intense appreciation for the crucial and significant roles they play in the lives of their family and their community. "They were soul mates, all of them. They were together to teach each other and then to carry those lessons over to their independent lives. They always would be linked by their love, by their memories and by the spiritual teachings that had tied them together."

Rivka Zakutinsky and Yaffa Leiba Gottlieb have formed an intimate relationship with these women, because they're not only the authors of this inspiring book published by Simon & Shuster, they're also members of the inner circle who gathers around Sarah's large, inviting table every Tuesday afternoon. There's a vacant seat by the window, so come pull-up a chair. As Sarah likes to point out, Hasidic philosophy suggests that "appetite comes with eating."

The Eternal Jewish Pilot Light

An extraordinary scene is currently being played out in homes all across Eastern Europe. As elderly gentiles are about to meet their maker, they are experiencing pangs of conscience and making deathbed confessions to the Jewish children they raised as their own. And so middle-aged adults who were brought up to attend church, practice Christian rites and celebrate Christian holidays are suddenly confronted with the revelation of their Jewish heritage.

"I kept trying to imagine what it would be like to wake up one day and find out you are not who you thought you were – and that your parents were not who they said they were," said Barbara Kessel, Director of Administration of the Board of Jewish Education of Greater New York.

Intrigued by the stories of people facing authentic "identity crises," she pursued the topic by placing ads in *The New York Times,* the *Jewish Press* and on the Internet. "I heard from former nuns, priests, Arabs, rabbis, neo-Nazis, African-Americans, prisoners. . . all kinds of people! After a year and a half I had interviewed more than two hundred people all over the globe."

The result of her research is *Suddenly Jewish: Jews Raised As Gentiles Discover Their Jewish Roots,* a compelling book of stories that aren't limited to children of the Holocaust, but include men and women from diverse backgrounds and cultures including crypto-Jews. "I heard from a woman who was cleaning out her attic in preparation of moving and found a tin box that contained her parents' *kesubah*. Others were adoptees who, in researching their roots, found their Jewish biological parents."

For Charlene Neely of San Diego, who grew up in a non-practicing Christian home, it was a 500-year journey. At age thirteen she felt there was a "spiritual hole" in her life and so she began to attend various services, but none felt comfortable. When her mother suggested that Charlene accompany her friend Susie to synagogue, the friend was puzzled why anyone would want to be Jewish if they didn't have to.

"But the minute I walked in it was like holy smokes, this was home!"

At age fifteen Charlene converted and eventually became a Jewish educator. Several years later when her son had to make a family tree for school, they researched the archives on her mother's side and found evidence that her ancestors had escaped the Spanish Inquisition. Mrs. Kessel was astounded to discover that eight percent of the people she interviewed had converted to Judaism long before they had any inkling they were of Jewish descent. "And scores more were drawn to Jews or Judaism without knowing why."

One woman majored in Jewish history. Another chose Israel for her junior college year abroad. "They just felt a pull that they could not ignore."

When she addresses groups around the country, Mrs. Kessel finds that audiences respond to these inspiring stories, which tug at your heartstrings, for two reasons. First, because people have a driving need to know who they are, where they come from and what their history is. Second, she believes people need spirituality in their lives and noted that after connecting to their roots many people "seem very relieved when they discover they belong to a tradition."

"This project took over my life for a year and a half," she laments good-naturedly. She would come home from work at the Board of Jewish Education, where she is responsible for the physical plant, personnel, public relations, purchasing and "anything else that starts with the letter P," throw a steak under the broiler and run to her computer or to the phone to conduct an interview. Twenty minutes later when the firemen would show up, her kids would open the door, "It's just our Mom again. She's writing a book."

Two of the people that she interviewed had a particularly profound effect on the author. One of them forms the Prologue in her book. "It's the story of a man whom I met in Israel on Kibbutz Sde Eliyahu. When he was about to take his vows for the priest-hood in France, the Cardinal told him his mother was Jewish and had survived the camps. He is now *Zayde* to several grandchil-dren."

The second was a Polish cleaning girl who cried every time she cooked *cholent* for her Jewish employer. "She didn't know why, but the smell threw her into a clinical depression," Mrs. Kessel recounts. She ultimately discovered that when her parents were being rounded up they gave their daughter to their non-Jewish neighbors. "Psychiatrists told me that the sense of smell is the most enduring sensory memory a person can have," said the author. "On a subconscious or pre-verbal level, this cleaning girl was re-membering her infancy in her Jewish home."

Psychologists, sociologists, rabbis and geneticists, whom Mrs. Kessel interviewed, explain this phenomenon as 'recovered memory.' Many of these people, they agree, probably had hints somewhere in their infancy or childhood that was awakened when they grew up and came into contact with other Jews.

"I had in the back of my mind the concept of the *yiddish neshoma* or the *pintele yid*," notes the author. "In fact, one person I interviewed said his rabbi told him he had a Jewish pilot light that just needed to be fanned into a blazing fire."

The Mysterious Profession of Rochelle Krich

A title like *Fertile Ground* and a cover illustration that depicts a lone flower with shallow roots might lead you to suuspect that this is a guide for the botanically challenged. But pay close attention, dear reader, because there is more to this book and its author than meets the eye.

"My father wore a *shtreimel* as a young man back in Poland, and the first thing he did after the war was to buy a pair of *tefillin*," according to best-selling mystery writer, Rochelle Krich.

Born in post-war Germany, Rochelle emigrated with her parents to America, where they were attracted to Lakewood, N.J. by the promise of the freedom and independence of life in the country. However, after a brief and unsuccessful stint on a chicken farm, the family settled in Crown Heights, Brooklyn, where Rochelle attended yeshiva and then went on to receive a B.A. from Stern College. When the west coast beckoned, the family moved to California and Rochelle earned her Masters Degree from U.C.L.A. She taught high school English for eighteen years and chaired the English department of Yeshiva University of Los Angeles High Schools, receiving the 1993 Milken Families Foundation Award for Distinguished Educator of the Year.

The Plot Thickens

"Although my own teachers told me I had talent and encouraged me to write" said Rochelle, "being a published author was always a fantasy. It was something that happened to other people." She didn't begin writing seriously until her youngest child was two and a half years old and started taking long naps. "My husband was very encouraging and told me to finally just sit down and write. I think he wants me to be rich and famous so he can retire and study Talmud all day," she noted good-naturedly.

Why whodunits? "I've always loved mysteries as a kid and as an adult. Even though I usually know who the killer is when I begin to write, I still like surprising myself. Half-way through writing one of my books I realized that I was about to kill the wrong person." For the author, who at one time considered going into law, writing provides her with the vicarious opportunity to take on the persona of a dedicated doctor, a resourceful lawyer and a fearless detective. In **Fertile Ground** (published by Avon Books, New York), set in the posh L.A. community of Westwood, Rochelle puts the medical profession under her microscope as a scandal shakes a fertility clinic accused of egg switching. Shades of the chicken farm?

"As the mother of six I never had difficulty conceiving. But I thought about all the women who do and asked myself, what happens if they're taken advantage of," said the author. She pointed out that the fertility industry is totally unregulated and until recently it was difficult to assign a price tag to an unfertilized egg. Egg stealing has just been deemed a felony, which is defined as stealing an item valued at $500 or more. The heroine of her book, a fertilization specialist who has strayed from her orthodox Jewish background, experiences a strong yearning to return which is complicated by the apparent murder of the clinic's director who is also her fiancée.

"My books deal increasingly with Jewish topics, because I'm more comfortable with airing my Jewishness," Rochelle said. The enthusiastic response to her books has proven there's definitely a reading public that's receptive to the Jewish themes she explores, with non-Jewish readers eager to learn about a culture so different than their own. "In writing about Jewish characters I feel a sense of responsibility because I'm aware that non-Jews are looking at my books through a different lens, therefore I'm careful not to present a negative view of Orthodox Judaism." According to Rochelle, in order to secure a *glatt hechsher* for her books, she consults with a rabbi.

In her acclaimed book, *Till Death Do Us Part,* Rochelle focused on the plight of the *agunah.* "Her husband refuses to give her a *Get* and won't let her go so I shoot him dead. It was a kind of satisfying moment," she admitted. She revealed that before her book came out, she received interesting letters from rabbis who tried to discourage her from publishing it for fear it was critical of *Halacha.* While more and more orthodox women are finding themselves in the situation she deals with in her book, Rochelle has been approached by reform and unaffiliated Jewish women who didn't realize, until they read her book, that any children they had after the divorce might have questionable status, according to Jewish law. These women now insist on obtaining a *Get* for legal reasons as well as out of a sense of closure.

Three Weddings and A Bar Mitzvah

"My kids have been wonderfully supportive in spite of the fact that I'm compulsive about my writing and do become absorbed in the world of characters that I create. At one time my daughter had twelve safety pins holding up her hem. I told her, learn to sew," she chuckled. Rochelle was under the gun this year, trying to meet her publisher's deadline for *Fertile Ground,* while at the same time plotting the weddings of three of her children and the Bar Mitzvah of her youngest son.

"Publishing is a very tough field. It's not about literature, it's about dollars and cents so I feel very fortunate that I have been published. I take nothing for granted and I thank *Hashem* for giving me a blessing," said Rochelle, the past editor of the Sisters In Crime Newsletter and former director of the National Board of Directors of the Mystery Writers of America and member of the American Crime Writers League.

Rochelle is currently working on her third book in the Jesse Drake Series, titled *Blood Money.* Jesse is a female homicide detective with the Los Angeles Police Department; the book deals with the contemporary themes of Nazi Gold and stolen art and incorporates the true-life wartime stories told to her by her father. One of her books, *Where's Mommy Now?,* was made into an HBO movie called *The Perfect Alibi* with Terry Garr. But will her father's dream of seeing a page-turner by his daughter turned into a hit movie directed by Steven Spielberg ultimately be fulfilled? The suspense builds.

VI

Leave Brooklyn? Fuggedaboudit!

*M*y *husband's two-year military obligation officially ended on the day the bicentennial began, July 4, 1976. We bid farewell to Maine and headed south, moving in temporarily with my parents, while we weighed the pros and cons of the various partnerships he was offered: a medical practice in an idyllic Connecticut town or another even further away in upstate New York.*

During our stay in Brooklyn my childhood friend, Phyllis Schweiger, recommended I see her obstretrician, David Kliot. When he heard our plans, he was shocked we would even think of living anywhere but his hometown, which he considered the center of the universe. My reason was less global. We were expecting our second child, so I felt reluctant to relocate far from my family. Dr. Kliot urged my husband to contact Dr. Sacharow, who was actively recruiting a partner for his very busy practice.

A medical practice in Brooklyn was definitely not my husband's first choice when he walked into the office of pediatrician Leonard Sacharow. Although they were completely different in background and temperament, something clicked from the moment the two men met.

Dr. Sacharow's only request was that my then non-observant husband refrain from working on the Sabbath. He agreed and they shook hands, a handshake that would last eighteen years.

Once we made the decision to remain in Brooklyn, the next step was finding a home for our growing family. During our first outing, the real estate agent showed us a small, attractive Tudor-style house that suited our needs. It was owned by a widow with grown children. Her name was Mrs. Hauser.

When I was a child growing up on West Third Street on the edge of Coney Island, the arrival of the cold season invariably brought Dr. Sol Hauser to our humble tenement apartment to cure our assorted winter ailments. The moment I heard his loud footsteps and his deep voice I began to howl, terrified of the dreaded shot that usually accompanied his visit. Although he was an "Americaner," my immigrant parents trusted him with the care of their children, because he spoke their language, respectfully communicating with them in Yiddish.

As I outgrew my childhood illnesses I began to see less of Dr. Hauser. And then when the developers came, demolishing all the tenements in our neighborhood to make way for the new high rises known as Trump Village, our family moved out of the area where Dr. Hauser had his office and we completely lost touch with him.

When she relocated to Florida, among the items Mrs. Hauser left behind for us was a mahogany dresser. The first night in my new home, I sat in my bedroom and stared for a very long time at the massive piece of furniture that once held the clothes of a very good man. I sensed that somewhere he must be smiling, pleased that the little girl he once cared for was now taking good care of his home.

Dr. Richard Golinko:
A Human Touch to the Cutting Edge

L ike a devoted father, Richard Golinko lovingly turns the pages of the photograph album, proudly pointing out the milestones in the lives of his children; births, Bar Mitzvahs, marriages. But as you look at their smiling faces and listen to their stories, you realize that each of these children is a living testament to Dr. Richard Golinko's leap of faith.

"This infant's mother was told to take her baby home to die because her medical center couldn't save his life," says Dr. Golinko. "Fortunately, she came to us instead." Today that baby is a beautiful teenager, because Richard Golinko had faith that in time medicine, doctors and technology would ultimately play catch up and solve the baby's problem.

As Director of Pediatric Cardiology and Professor of Pediatrics at Mount Sinai Medical Center, and the Senior Pediatric Cardiologist in New York City, Dr. Golinko has been solving problems of the heart during a long and distinguished career that has spanned decades. "I've grown up in the field so I've had the privilege of seeing many innovations over the past 40 years."

During the almost quarter of a century he served as Director of Pediatrics and Pediatric Cardiology at Brookdale Hospital in Brooklyn, where my husband is an attending physician, Dr. Golinko was responsible for introducing a wide range of innovative and diagnostic treatment techniques; the first to use medications like prostaglandin to treat patients; the first to use interventional cardiac catheterization procedures, such as balloon dilation of obstructed valves; the first to employ two-dimensional echocardiography, a sonar imaging technique in utero.

The $2 Million Wish List

But it was back in 1985 that Dr. Golinko accepted his greatest challenge, to save the Department of Pediatric Cardiology at Mount Sinai Medical Center in Manhattan and establish a premier center for infants, children and young adults afflicted with heart defects. It wasn't an easy decision.

"I had mixed feelings about leaving Brookdale at that stage in my career," he admits. "But I knew the Pediatric Program at this world renowned Jewish hospital was in danger of closing and I felt a real emotional attachment and commitment to the department where I had interned in Pediatric Cardiology."

Dr. Golinko graduated from Cornell and New York Medical College and after interning at Mount Sinai, he did his residency at Philadelphia Children's Hospital and his fellowships at Harvard Medical School, Boston Children's Hospital and The Albert Einstein College of Medicine. His wife, Joan, who always understood his dedication, encouraged him to follow his heart. "I saw this as my opportunity to give back to the place that had meant so much to me personally and professionally." His decision to bring his expertise and his talents to Mount Sinai ultimately brought the Medical Center to the forefront of Pediatric Cardiology.

As he proudly surveys the exciting state-of-the-art facility he has created, Dr. Golinko recalls his conversation twelve years ago with the Board of Trustees and the President of the hospital when they first asked, "What do you need to get the job done?" For the answer he turned to his long-time colleague and friend, Dr. Randall Griepp, who had been recruited at the same time to be chairman of Cardio thoracic Surgery. Dr. Griepp pioneered a number of surgical procedures in both adults and children, including the first successful heart transplant in a child.

"It was right after Yom Kippur that Randall and I sat down and came up with a $2 million dollar wish list, which included an all out effort to recruit the best and the brightest," said Dr. Golinko. "I insisted on bringing in a group of young, well-trained Pediatric

Cardiologists with the kind of expertise required to create a major diagnostic and treatment center for pediatric cardiology and surgery in this region. Humanity is a major criteria for me. I wanted a staff that was sensitive and caring about a patient's needs. And so I always asked myself, is this a person I want to live with?"

And so he began to put together his dream team. From Children's Hospital in Boston came Dr. Ira A. Parness, an expert in echocardiography, to be the Associate Director of Pediatric Cardiology and Director of Pediatric Echocardiography. He brought in Dr. Anthony Rossi from Children's Hospital in Philadelphia and appointed him Medical Director of the Pediatric Cardiology Intensive Care Unit and the head of the pediatric heart transplant patient program. Dr. Robert J. Sommer was appointed Director of Pediatric Cardiology Catheterization.

Also from Boston Children's Hospital came Dr. Steven B. Fishberger, Assistant Professor of Pediatrics, whose expertise is evaluating and treating arrhythmia with non-invasive methods. From the prestigious Institute for Molecular Genetics in Houston he recruited Dr. Bruce D. Gelb, Associate Professor of Pediatrics and Human Genetics with expertise in the genetic aspects of congenital heart disease as well as various inherited metabolic heart conditions. Also recruited was Dr. Wyman Lai, an expert in congenital heart disorders, who had trained with Hillel Lax, the leading Cardiac surgeon in the world.

Moshe Comes To Mount Sinai

It was this team that proved crucial in saving the life of a newborn infant, named Moshe, who was born with hypoplastic left heart syndrome, meaning that all of the left heart structures in his heart were severely underdeveloped. In a sense, he was born with only half a heart. Most children with this syndrome die during the first few weeks of life. "He was diagnosed on Shabbos," says Moshe's mother. "We were referred to several hospitals and had to decide quickly where to take him for treatment. We have never regretted our decision to come to Mount Sinai."

Before Mount Sinai assembled its team of congenital heart specialists in the late 1980s, no child had ever survived surgery for this disorder in New York City. Led by Dr. Wyman Lai, the Cardiologists developed the treatment plan and Moshe underwent his first open heart surgery at just 12 days of age. He was to undergo two more major operations. During the last, the disturbance of the heart rhythm was so severe that all previous reported therapies proved unsuccessful and his doctor was forced to develop a new experimental treatment that was so successful Moshe recovered completely.

The treatment will be published in a prestigious medical journal. But the real success story is that the infant, who was born with a lethal heart problem, just celebrated his 5th birthday. "Moshe attends kindergarten and runs and plays just like any child," says his mother. The picture in his photo album reveals a cheerful, normal looking little boy.

Dr. Golinko replaces the album on its special shelf in his personal office. While the Pediatric ICU and the Catheter Lab provide patients with the cutting edge in technological facilities, the ever present human touch is evident everywhere you look in Richard Golinko's office. Posing against a wall, you're greeted by the familiar images of Mickey Mouse, Pinocchio and Donald Duck, masquerading as giant marionettes.

"I'd like to share with you a moving story about these marionettes," Dr. Golinko offers. "During my first week here at Mount Sinai I saw a twenty-three year old from Norway with a complex heart problem, a two instead of a four chambered heart. When he entered my office and saw the marionettes he began to cry." Dr. Golinko becomes visibly emotional as he relates the story. "The young man realized that when he was seven years old he had been brought to see me at Brookdale Hospital. He vividly remembered how thrilled he felt when I let him play with the marionettes. Shortly after his visit, his father moved the family to Norway and he never dreamt that he would ever see the marionettes again."

Another wall, another *midrash*. "One of my patients, an eight year old boy who was suffering from a serious life-threatening heart disease, mentioned that he was a Cub Scout. I told him that I had been an Eagle Scout and that when he becomes one, too, I want to be there to pin his badge on him." That little boy is now a married man and the Eagle Scout Badge that Dr. Golinko was privileged to pin on him today occupies a place of honor alongside his numerous awards and degrees.

It's hard to miss the giant stethoscope that decorates another wall. It was a gift from Dr. Golinko's three daughters, Lori, Nancy and Susan, and is inscribed with the words *"To Our Loving Dad, whose big heart has helped so many little hearts."* It is an appropriate symbol for the larger than life accomplishments of Dr. Richard Golinko. And yet, he is the first to recognize the limitations of human endeavors. "Today we can repair the tiniest parts of the tiniest hearts, but there is just so much that I, as a doctor, can personally do. I believe in God and I know that ultimately, the rest is in his hands."

Although he may not describe himself as an outwardly religious man, Dr. Richard Golinko's dedication to the sanctity of the lives that have been entrusted to him, reveals a man of remarkable faith.

This Old Stone House

Lexington and Concord are familiar names when it comes to the Revolutionary War, but Brooklyn? "Few people are aware that the **Battle of Brooklyn** was the first, largest and most crucial battle fought between the British Army and the newly formed army of the United States of America," according to Herb Yellin, customs attorney and noted authority on the Battle of Brooklyn. During his fascinating presentation on **"Jewish Americans and the Revolutionary War,"** you could almost hear the walls of the landmark **Old Stone House,** located at Fifth Avenue and Third Street, echoing Mr. Yellin's tales of courage and intrigue.

On the morning of August 27, 1776, the British had armed themselves with a light cannon in the second floor of the Old Stone House from where they attacked the colonists who valiantly led charge after charge against the building located in the heart of Park Slope.

"Just like in Maccabean times, once again it was a case of the few against the many, when a small band of 400 Americans fought against 2,000 British and Hessian troops," Mr. Yellin noted. Although they succeeded in clearing the house, their losses were so severe they were forced to surrender. But their brave efforts allowed the American army to regroup and gave their morale a necessary boost.

As members of *Shomer Shabbos* Boy Scout Troop 611 listened intently, Mr. Yellin introduced the major Jewish patriots who figured so prominently in the battle for independence. Among the 100 Jews who served in the American army was Colonel Solomon Bush, who fought in the Battle of Brooklyn and was later promoted to lieutenant-colonel and made deputy adjutant-general of the Pennsylvania militia. He was the highest ranking Jewish officer in the American army. The only statue erected to a Jewish revolutionary soldier was built to honor Frances Salvador of South Carolina, who was the first and only Jewish legislator to serve during the war. The statue still stands in Charleston.

A name familiar to many Americans who have studied the Revolution is Haym Solomon, who emigrated here from Poland in 1772. He served in many capacities, including as a spy for the American army. Condemned to death by the British, he fled to France where he became involved in brokering promissory notes "and so he is therefore remembered for keeping the American economy afloat when others thought American money was not worth the paper it was printed on," Mr. Yellin said.

It was the Jewish merchants who had a direct impact on the war effort as they funded the American privateer ships to capture British ships, run the British blockade and land materials for America's army.

During the informative and entertaining **Old Stone House** presentation, Brooklyn educator and historian, Ron Schweiger added this bit of folk history to the house's notoriety when he revealed that "at one time the house and land was the site of the ball field of the Brooklyn club of the National Baseball League. When electric trolleys began to zoom down Brooklyn streets, the residents of Brooklyn became known as trolley *dodgers*, and that's how Brooklyn's famous ball team got its name."

VII

The British Invade Brooklyn—Again!

*T*he modern day invasion of Brooklyn bore little resemblance to the original 1776 onslaught. Armed with videocams and boom mikes instead of muskets, their target was the Winner House on Seabreeze Avenue. But this time the Brits were conquered by a writer brandishing a pen and a dynamic rebbetzin who could wield a cleaver in the kitchen as expertly as she gave a lesson in Torah study.

As a result of the popularity of our Jewish cooking video, **"A Taste Of Shabbos,"** Esther Winner's reputation as a gourmet cook made it all the way across the Atlantic. So it's not surprising that when British television teamed up with PBS for a series on multicultural cuisines called **The United Tastes of America**, Esther and her children were the natural choice for the segment on the traditional Jewish family. I joined the project as a script and production assistant.

As the film crew transformed Esther's kitchen into their studio we had our own agenda. Determined to convey to the audience that "Judaism is more than just chicken soup" we managed to sprinkle in a little ritual with every recipe and seasoned the program with much more than the joy of cooking Jewish.

When the exciting day of filming came to an end there was more good news for the dynamic duo. **"Miracle On Seabreeze Avenue,"** the autobiographical documentary I had written and produced about my personal journey, with a film crew consisting of my brother Milton and Esther's son Avraham, was selected to receive the **Brooklyn Women's History Month Video Award**.

During the awards ceremony on March 10, 1997, held in the historic Borough Hall building, I addressed the audience, which included family and friends, and marveled at my transformation from an impoverished refugee to the wife, mother and career woman I had become. And I gratefully acknowledged the major role Brooklyn had played in my intellectual and spiritual growth, as it had for so many other immigrants.

The Roots of Success

I watch the little children navigate the intricate world of the beach. As one child digs a hole in the sand, her friend pours in a bucket of water, creating mud; the chemistry of play. Since first meeting in kindergarten, my son, Andrew, and Ronit would share pail and shovel for several years in their ongoing summer dialogue. And as the simple language of children gradually developed into a complex vocabulary, who could have predicted that this miraculous process of learning would one day lead to the daunting **"Experimental Investigation of the Solubility of Gibbsite at 25 Degrees Centigrade."**

This is the language of the scientist that Ronit has become and her research into trace aluminum in water has earned her a place as one of Midwood High School's thirteen semi-finalists in the prestigious nationwide 1998 Westinghouse Science Talent Search. "Acid rain causes a higher concentration of this potentially toxic form of aluminum in water and has been linked to Alzheimer's disease," according to Ronit. Her research has profound implications for the environment and for human beings.

"I've always been fascinated by chemistry. I'm interested in how humans and organisms interact with the environment and I plan to become an environmental chemist" she revealed. Encouraged by her Israeli-born mother, Ronit devoted over 30 hours per week as well as her summers to her research at the Brooklyn College Geochemistry Lab. She is also the editor-in-chief of Midwood's Biology Magazine, a member of the math team and the yearbook staff, and she takes piano and karate lessons, attends services every Shabbos at East Midwood Jewish Center's Young People's Synagogue and the Talmud Torah High School each Sunday.

The Recipe For Success

"Resources we don't have, our labs are outdated and the students were forced to travel to better equipped facilities to do their research, so why did Midwood High School in Brooklyn have the greatest number of semi-finalists in America?" asks principal Lewis Frohlich. "First and foremost, I have to give credit to the teachers who work well beyond the 6 hour and 20 minute schedule."

The Shomer Shabbos principal describes himself as a product of the public schools, Seward Park H.S. on the lower east side, and emphasizes their great potential. "My goal is to provide a quality education in spite of Midwood's physical shortcomings." But what the school doesn't offer in physical facilities, he pointed out, it more than makes up in a curriculum that is "imaginative, challenges students, encourages critical thinking skills, ethics, research techniques, lab techniques and gives students a well-rounded education."

"One major part of the recipe for success is that these students are willing to work above and beyond what's called for," said Jay Touger, who along with Mitchel Kalmus and Stanley Shapiro, are the three advisors who have guided the students in their research. The students are not only intellectually gifted but each one talks seriously about his or her goal for the future. And as I listen to the six Jewish students talk about their backgrounds, I hear a common theme running through each of their stories. The immigrant experience has had a profound influence on each of these children who represent the diversity of the Jewish people on a global scale.

Anna Kundel only arrived in America in 1992 from Moldava in the Soviet Union. Her entire family left prestigious jobs and made sacrifices so that Anna, an only child, would have the opportunities that eluded them. "My grandparents, who are religious, live with us and I'm very close to them," said Anna who plans to attend medical school. She pointed out that when her own mother wanted to go into medicine in the Soviet Union, she experienced discrimination. When Anna began to investigate topics for research, she was surprised to learn that New York was one of the major cities affected by diseases transmitted by mosquito. Her research into creating a biological pesticide may one day be used to eradicate mosquitoes naturally, without the use of chemicals that are harmful to the environment. It may also provide a cure for cancer by stimulating the cells to kill themselves.

It's All In The Family

When Hope Rachel Garner took a trip to Portugal recently, she was overwhelmed by the sight that greeted her when she visited a Temple. The building was completely surrounded by a wall, totally shielding it from view and therefore from harm. That sight crystallized for Hope the persecutions her Sephardic ancestors must have endured. "During the Inquisition, my family escaped to Goa, a Portuguese colony in India. My grandmother returned to Portugal and that's where my mother was born."

Although Hope's grandparents were religious, her mother had to attend a strict Catholic school to get a good education. Since her mother was interested in medicine, she was forced to immigrate to America at the age of 19, because women, especially Jewish women, had very few opportunities in the medical field in Portugal.

"My mom always stressed academics and encouraged me to take advantage of the opportunities here," said Hope. With a mother, who's a psychiatrist, and a father a radiologist, it's not surprising that Hope is interested in pursuing a medical career. Using the facilities at the SUNY Health Sciences Center, Hope altered gene expression in leukemia cells to see if she could suppress the metastasis, research that could some day lead to a cure.

"Both of my parents are involved in the educational field and have steered me towards the sciences," acknowledged Jared Ravi Jagdeo. His mother's family has roots in the Caribbean and Europe, while his father traces his ancestry to India. Jared attended Sephardic Yeshiva and the East Midwood Jewish Center Talmud

Torah H.S. and he continues to study with Rabbi Kurzrock of Young Israel of Kensington.

Jared praised Midwood High School for cementing his devotion to the sciences by helping him develop the critical skills for the development of a scientist. For his project he identified protein on the surface of cells which become tumors. The future applications of his research may result in the identification of the early stages of cancer before the tumor metastasizes. Jared's goal is to go into medicine and has his sights set on Harvard, Yale and M.I.T.

The present method for cleaning up soil pollution, a major environmental hazard, involves the costly and harmful excavation of the land. For his Westinghouse project Hesky Fisher researched a method for harnessing bacteria to do all the work. "I don't remember a time when I wasn't interested in math and science. I was always trying to figure out how things work," said Hesky, who was a student at Krasna Yeshiva in Williamsburg and attended the Bobover Yeshiva in Boro Park before transferring to Midwood because of its intense science program.

His Israeli-born mother was enthusiastic about his interest in science. But in order to qualify he had to take physics in summer school at Stuyvesant H.S. "I'm interested in environmental engineering and Midwood has provided a very nurturing environment. The teachers are very understanding and everyone works around the religious holidays." Hesky is the president of the Jewish club and he continues his religious studies daily with one on one learning.

Svetlana Zapolskaya has a sweet sounding voice without the hint of an accent so it's hard to believe that she only came to America in 1991 from the Soviet Union. In spite of widespread anti-Semitism, Svetlana's father was so outstanding in his field that he was offered the presidency of a diesel company in Riga. But because he knew the opportunities for his only child were so limited, the family made the decision to leave.

"My grandmother, who died four years ago, had a great influence on me," said Svetlana. "She was a religious woman and she brought me up."

The topic for her research project came as a result of volunteering in the Psychiatric-Geriatric facility where her mother works. It was here that Svetlana saw first hand the devastating affects of Alzheimer's. She designed a diagnostic apparatus to diagnose Alzheimer's Disease. "Sometimes it can take up to 15 years to diagnose the disease, but one day I hope a physician will be able to make the diagnosis in his office as a result of this research," said Svetlana. Her goal is to be a physical therapist.

Children of the Inquisition, children of the Holocaust, children of the Revolution, the exodus continues. It's the same scenario that has been played out on different stages throughout history. And as these remarkable children conquer disease and save the environment and cure cancer, they will fulfill the hopes of generations that have dared to share their dreams with them.

Angels of Mercy

Not all angels commute via their wings. Some ride the city bus, as Margie Halbfinger found out that fateful day when two angels descended from the B-36 and came to her rescue on a stormy Brooklyn street.

Margie's ordeal began uneventfully with an excursion to her neighborhood Keyfood Supermarket. She filled her shopping cart with groceries and began what she expected to be a pleasant walk home, when a sudden storm appeared out of nowhere. "It started to rain and the wind was so strong I could hardly walk," Margie remembers.

Halfway across a busy intersection, the wind knocked her over and ripped the cart from her hands. As cars whizzed by and "every second seemed like an hour," she suddenly felt two strong arms surround her and heard a reassuring voice say, "Don't worry, it's all right. I'll help you."

Margie's voice quivered with emotion, as she recounted the event. "He held me in his arms and didn't let go of me. He walked me to my building and all the way home he encouraged me and reassured me that he would not let go until we got safely home. When we got upstairs to my apartment, he made sure I was okay and didn't leave until a neighbor I called arrived."

Who were these "angels," as she describes them, who flew to Margie Halbfinger's aide? They were thirteen year-old Brady Gonzalez and his eleven year-old sister Jaynnie. The children were on their way home from an after-school program, when Brady looked out the bus window and spotted Margie. At first, the driver refused to let them off, but Brady persisted. What made him leave the safety of the bus in the middle of a storm?

"When I saw this lady lying on the street, I knew I had to go help her," he said. "It could have been my mother or my grandmother who was in trouble and if I didn't do anything I would always feel guilty."

This might have been just an ordinary "boy helps lady in distress" story had it ended there. But Margie Shenkin Halbfinger is no ordinary lady but an extraordinarily independent woman of remarkable strength and character who has made many journeys in her ninety-one years. But for Margie, that short trip from the supermarket to her home had seemed like the longest of her life.

Grateful for the exceptional kindness these two children had shown her, she immediately sent off two long letters to their school. The principal was so impressed by the children's behavior, he held an assembly in their behalf. Margie attended and thanked them publicly, because she felt it was "important that the other children should know that a good deed is appreciated and remembered." And it didn't surprise her when she learned that as a fourth-grader, Brady had won first prize in an essay writing contest. The topic was the Holocaust.

Had the children *just* rescued Margie and the school *just* held an assembly in their honor, that would have been enough as the familiar Passover song says. But the story doesn't end there, because also present at the assembly that day was Rachelle Ettman, whose parents are survivors of the Holocaust. Rachelle is a Field Director for the **Council For Unity,** a school-based organization that promotes unity among different racial and ethnic groups.

The traits these children demonstrated were exactly what the council had been striving for, so when she learned that Brady Gonzalez was a member, Rachelle was determined that he and his sister should be honored at the council's annual Student Congress Appreciation Awards Evening in 1998. And so once again fate brought together Brady and Jaynnie from Coney Island and Margie Halbfinger from Brighton Beach. Chase Bank, an ardent supporter of the Council who sponsored the Awards evening, welcomed the group of honorees and their families to the bank's elegant headquarters on Park Avenue in Manhattan.

In that rarefied atmosphere of the 49th floor, framed by the Chrysler Building on her left and the Empire State building on her right, the former school secretary who remembers when Brooklyn was a wilderness and cows and nanny goats roamed in her backyard, spoke quietly and with dignity. She hugged her "angels" and thanked God for her good fortune and for allowing her to participate in this special event.

The young members of the Council whose families had emigrated from Europe, the Middle East, Asia and Africa, listened with rapt attention to the great-grandmother from Russia whose life had spanned the twentieth century as she praised the parents and teachers who "worked so hard to raise such kind and caring children."

Dr. Leonard Sacharow:
The Gentle Giant

A small basket filled with lollipops sat on the synagogue seat of a very large man. It was placed there by his family in memory of a man who kept candy in his tallis bag to give to the little children on Shabbos so the Torah would taste sweet. This devotion to children was the essence of Dr. Leonard Sacharow, a beloved pediatrician who died on May 9, 1995 and was buried in Eretz Yisrael.

When family, friends and colleagues of Dr. Sacharow came together for an evening of remembrance in his synagogue, the Sephardic Congregation of Long Beach, New York, they honored a man who never sought honors and conveyed their love for a man who was a master at conversing with the smallest child or an elderly grandparent. Each person who spoke had their own inspiring story to tell about an extraordinary human being whose greatest satisfaction came from helping and healing.

Born in 1937 in Dublin, where his parents owned a grocery business, Leonard Sacharow was encouraged to study medicine by his father, who impressed upon him the importance of serving humanity. He attended Trinity College and completed his medical internship in Ireland.

Appointed Chief Resident of Pediatrics at Brooklyn Jewish Hospital, he later became an attending physician at Brookdale Medical Center with his own private practice in Brooklyn, which became well-known for the support and encouragement he offered young mothers and his humanistic approach to medical care.

During his tribute to his partner of eighteen years, Richard Schwimmer described their unique relationship. "When Lenny and I shook hands that handshake was our agreement to become partners. It was all that I needed, because I could sense immediately, just as his patients did, that this was a man you could trust. His only stipulation was that I agree not to work on the Sabbath. The word *Shabbos* was not a part of my vocabulary, yet. Lenny and I finally did get around to signing a formal agreement ten years later. By then I had learned quite a lot about Shabbos as well as what it meant to be a *mensch* from the man who could have invented the word."

He went on to share some of the stories about Dr. Sacharow's dedication to his patients that had become legend. "One mother told me that when Lenny made a house call at midnight to examine her cranky infant and saw how exhausted she was he insisted that she get some rest and proceeded to put the baby to sleep himself. This compassion and devotion is not taught in medical school. It comes from the heart and Lenny Sacharow had a big heart.

"Another patient described to me the first time she visited our office. After offering the new mother valuable advice on how to care for her infant, Lenny then gave her pointers on how to make the best gefilte fish."

Dr. Sacharow's greatest satisfaction came when his patients grew up and returned to him with babies of their own. As a patient wrote in one of the hundreds of letters the family received from devoted parents and children, "I was never afraid of the gentle giant."

He was married for 28 years to Cecelia Meyers Sacharow, who, together with their four children and the generous support of hundreds of devoted patients and friends, have built a playground in memory of Dr. Sacharow and his parents at the **Count Me In** school for the developmentally disabled in Netanya, Israel. And it is there, Cecelia will tell you, where you will find Lenny's gentle neshama watching over the little children.

VIII

Converts, Baalei Teshuvah and My Mid-life Spiritual Awakening

*M*any of my most meaningful interviews have been with converts, remarkable people who have taken upon themselves the mitzvahs many of us take for granted. I have spoken with frum rebbetzins who were brought up as devout Christians. I have met Christians who discovered they were Jews. The love and enthusiasm they display for a life of Torah inevitably invigorates and revitalizes the Jewish community that embraces them.

I found the stories of Jews who ultimately found their way back to their heritage equally compelling. For one baal teshuvah it was the powerful influence of a spiritual leader that inspired his return. For another it was the sound of two simple words, "Good Shabbos."

I have spoken with a middle-aged FFB (frum from birth), who told me she planned to study at Neve Yerushalayim. Puzzled, I asked her why since this was a seminary for women who were just beginning on their path to observance. "I want to feel like a baal teshuvah," she confided, meaning that she longed to reconnect with the intensity someone feels who has only recently reconnected with their heritage.

I have watched a group of women, who are members of a reform synagogue on Long Island, excited to be braiding their own challah for the first time in their lives. And when they are told there is a mitzvah to make a blessing over the challah, they are eager to learn how to perform it.

And into this landscape of wandering Jews, following a complex itinerary on their sacred journey to their roots, I must include my own story. My mid-life spiritual awakening ultimately led me to the East, not to a secluded mountaintop but to a crowded wall.

Being And Becoming In Jerusalem

The delicate red string encircles the wrist of my right hand. "Look for the old woman on your way to the wall," my friend, Elise, had instructed me before I left for Israel. And so I was prepared with *tzedakah*, when I saw her approach, clutching a fistful of strings. However, nothing could have prepared me for the many blessings I would receive during my sojourn in Jerusalem.

Israel had been beckoning to me for sometime. But it wasn't until I read the itinerary from the *Isralight Institute* that I made up my mind that it was time to return. My last trip had been in 1971, when I was a young bride, a typical tourist who had come to check out the sights. But by the summer of '99 both Israel and I had changed dramatically. I was returning as an observant Jewish woman accompanied by the youngest of my three children, my nineteen year-old son Andrew. When I reassured him that this type of program involved no homework and no exams, he was enthusiastic about the trip, especially since it also gave him the opportunity to see his best friend, Rafi, who was spending the year studying at the Ohr Somayach Seminary.

Isralight offered a ten day program of learning and touring that promised a "profound Jewish experience that is contemporary, open-minded, spiritual, relevant and inspiring." It turned out to be all that and so much more. From the very first morning when Andrew and I passed through the Jaffa Gate, we felt Jerusalem reach out and envelop us. As we navigated the narrow streets of the old city in search of Misgav Ladach 25, we encountered Greek

Orthodox clergymen, Muslim storekeepers, Christian pilgrims and fellow Jews who were dressed in every type of head covering and skirt length, representing the entire spectrum of the Diaspora experience.

Seated in the *Isralight* building, a 900-year old crusader edifice overlooking the Western Wall, I found that our group, ranging in age from eighteen to sixty, was equally diverse in their religious and geographical backgrounds. Sylvie had come all the way from California, leaving her job in the Silicon Valley to explore her Jewish identity. Brad, who spent several weeks volunteering on a kibbutz, was from Missouri. Two young women, Tamar and Melissa, had made the trek all the way from Australia. Janice and Shelly, wives and mothers like me, were from Michigan. Ari, from Vancouver, had already experienced the religious enclave of Crown Heights, Brooklyn. Tammy and Paul, a young married couple from Florida, had come to learn together.

Donna, Moshe, Bobbi and Dana were part of a group of single New Yorkers who had come with Rabbi Yitz and Sharon Motechin of Kehilat Jeshurun in Manhattan. Daniel and Lisa and their parents from Queens were repeaters. They had sampled a taste of *Isralight* when they sat in on a class during their trip to Israel a year ago and came back for the full menu. And Roni, originally from Santa Barbara, now resided in the old city just steps from the Institute. What had brought us all together? Each one had come searching for that link, the crucial connection between our ancient heritage and our contemporary lives.

Rabbi David Aaron, the visionary who is the Founder and Dean of the thirteen-year old *Isralight Institute,* is acutely aware of this profound yearning that the soul has to reconnect to its source. The son of Holocaust survivors, he grew up in a secular home in Toronto. His journey began as a young man when he started to observe Shabbat and "realized this was a powerful way to live my life." A dynamic speaker who has provided spiritual guidance to celebrities Kirk Douglas and Goldie Hawn, Rabbi Aaron now resides with his wife, Chana, and their six children in a home inside the walls of the old city.

Our introduction to Jerusalem actually began beneath the

city. *Isralight* had arranged for Jeff Seidel, tour guide extraordinaire, to lead us through the newly excavated tunnels that date back to the Hashmonean period. As we explored the tunnels that run beneath the Kotel we discovered that the part of the Western Wall that is visible above ground is only a very small segment of the total wall which is actually a third of a mile long. It was an appropriate introduction to the paradox that is Judaism. God is within this world and at the same time beyond.

Who you are, your intelligence and your talents, is God's gift to you. Who you become is your gift to God, Rabbi Aaron pointed out during one of his riveting classes. Therefore it is up to you "to take your fate and turn it into destiny."

How do we accomplish this? "You can't grow unless you make choices and the Torah is our guide to growth," he suggests. The world of growing, of "becoming," is an endless journey.

My own journey began several years before at the Shabbat table of Rabbi Zushe and Rebbetzin Esther Winner. For me Shabbat was also the key which unlocked the door to exploring my heritage. My first Shabbat experience in Jerusalem, I would discover by the end of the week, would open yet another door.

Our stay in Israel coincided with the 17th of Tammuz, the beginning of the three weeks before Tish B'Av; Rav Binny Freedman, the Educational Director of *Isralight,* took us on a tour of the old city. Originally from Manhattan, Rav Binny made *aliyah* when he was eighteen and continued his studies at Yeshivat Har Etzion. He now lives with his wife and children in Efrat. An expert storyteller, Rav Binny loves books and music, and so he always has both at his side, a guitar to accompany us in a *niggun* and the appropriate text to inspire and connect us to our past. When he read to us from the writings of the historian, Josephus, describing the siege of Jerusalem, we could almost hear the Roman battering rams pounding on the gates.

As I became immersed in the history, the philosophy and the ancient texts, I found myself on a continuous spiritual high. During lunch breaks I stood on the roof of the *Isralight* building and inhaled the view. Below me was the *Kotel,* to my right the Mount of Olives and to my left Hebrew University and Hadassah

Hospital. I took photographs. I took movies. I couldn't get enough of the sights and sounds of Jerusalem. I marveled, as I strolled down to the *Kotel*, that these past few years I had been facing east and now I was east. And then from out of nowhere, a blessing. When I ran into my son at the Wailing Wall, he mentioned rather casually, that he had just put on *Tefillin*.

After a morning of classes, Rav Binny took us on a tour of the Elah Valley and Gush Etzion which had been attacked in 1948 during the War of Independence. Although the women and children were evacuated, the Jordanians had massacred all the men who were trying to defend the settlement, which was also strategic to the defense of Jerusalem. The territory was recaptured during the 1967 Six-Day War and the adult children of the original settlers returned and rebuilt Kfar Etzion, which is now a thriving kibbutz.

Our next stop was Rav Binny's alma mater, Yeshivat Har Etzion, where he shared with us heroic stories of classmates who had served with him in the army. As we stood in the *Beit Hamidrash*, enveloped by the sound of learning, I realized that Israel's most valuable resource were these unique people who embodied the qualities of soldier, scholar and builder. That's the kind of man my father, David Zegerman z"l, was — scholar and a builder who dreamt of building Eretz Yisroel. The only one in his immediate family to survive the Holocaust, he had planned to make aliyah. But when my mother's only surviving brother, Moishe, immigrated to America she insisted we follow and so my father never saw his dream come true.

Shabbat. I stroll down to the Kotel Plaza which is filled with thousands of Jews from all over the world. Jerusalem feels like a college town. It is the first weekend in July and students, who have come to participate in the many programs Israel has to offer, are spending their first Shabbat in the old city ". . .*and gather us together from the four corners of the earth.*" (*Shmoneh Esrei* prayer.)

As we welcome in Shabbat at **Isralight**, Rabbi Aaron suggests that this is a time for us to just "be" and not "become," and so he asks us to close our eyes and allow ourselves to feel grateful. He begins to sing a *niggun* and my father's face suddenly appears before me. I am overwhelmed with emotion as I realize that the little tunes, the *lidderlach* that my father often sang whenever he was happy, were actually *niggunim.*

As we join hands and ascend to the rooftop I am singing and dancing and crying with joy as I feel my father rejoicing with us. *"Build me a house and I will dwell in them."* (Exodus 25:8) My father's neshama has finally come to dwell in Yerushalayim.

Being And Becoming In Jerusalem: Part II

I had often heard Jerusalem described as a timeless and ageless city. But it wasn't until I experienced this mystical phenomenon for myself that I understood how easily you become immersed in a different dimension when you enter Jerusalem.

I had chosen to stay in the Dan Pearl Hotel just outside the Jaffa Gate, an ideal location because it was easily accessible to the Isralight Institute located in the old city and to bustling Ben Yehuda Street. In real time my nineteen year-old son, Andrew, and I had been in Israel for just a week when we went out to dinner one evening with several members of our group. Although I was about twice their age, somehow the generation gap had narrowed considerably after studying the ancient texts together in a building that was over 900 years old, in a city *"where a thousand years. . .are but a bygone yesterday."* (Psalm 90)

Dinner lasted past midnight so Andrew and I escorted Sylvie, one of the young women, back to the old city where she was staying in the Isralight dorm. As we navigated the dark, narrow streets, suddenly I saw a familiar figure walking towards me. It was my husband, Richard. He had come to Israel to join us for the second part of the program but when he arrived at our hotel we weren't there so he set out to find us. And he did. That's Israel. Inevitably you will find what you're looking for, whether it's people or answers.

Although my father z"l had dreamt of making aliyah after surviving the Holocaust, fate intervened and brought our family to America instead. Now, more than fifty years later, I brought his youngest grandson to Israel to connect my father's legacy with our own lives. Connecting. That was the operative word for our experience in Israel, the crossroads where past and present converge and the ancient and modern weave an intricate daily tapestry.

I marveled at the different people who meandered into the *Isralight* building each day, constantly reminding us of the world that existed beyond its walls. Lisa Castleman, an anchor at Fox News, had come to do a story on the political and economic scene and sat in on several Isralight classes. Bruce Burger, the singer and composer of the hit "Rebbe Soul" was seeking inspiration for a new album and joined our group for an impromptu sing-along. One morning I looked up from a page of Talmud we were studying to see Rabbi Avi Weiss of Riverdale *kvelling* as he listened intently to the class being given by his former student, Rav Binny Freedman, the Educational Director of Isralight.

The diversity of the students was echoed by the diversity of the Isralight Institute staff. There were the FFBs *(frum from birth)* like Binny Freedman and Program Coordinator Shprintzee Herskovitz who had grown up on the Upper West Side of Manhattan. Then there were those who had come from a completely assimilated background, including Rabbi David Aaron, originally from Toronto, Canada, the visionary Founder and Director of the Institute. Kerry Behrendt had attended the High School of Music and Art in NYC and majored in Psychology at the University of Michigan. Originally raised in a Reform home, she received her first introduction to traditional Judaism when she came to study at Isralight several years ago. Today she is in charge of Recruitment and it was her enthusiasm and eagerness to answer all my questions that encouraged me to join the program.

Rabbi Natan Lopes Cardozo, whose ancestors were originally exiled from Spain during the Inquisition, grew up in a secular home in Amsterdam and became a Professor of Philosophy. A late-bloomer, he was drawn to Judaism in middle-age and ultimately attended Yeshiva and became an ordained Rabbi. He now teaches Torah with fervor and a charming Dutch accent. Gila Manolson, author of *The Magic Touch,* was a feminist educated at

Yale, but today she lectures on men, women and relationships and lives in Jerusalem with her husband and six children.

The New York Connection

When I first heard Rebbetzin Tziporah Heller speak in New York City several years ago, I never envisioned myself sitting in her classroom in Jerusalem. But one morning, during an *Isralight* break, I took the opportunity to combine a visit with an old friend who lived in Har Nuf and a class with Mrs. Heller. Surrounded by young women who had come from all over the world to learn from this inspiring teacher, I was delighted to finally experience the *Neve* I had heard so much about.

Another New York connection. When I met Rabbi David Geffen during a talk he gave at Aish Hatorah in Manhattan, he graciously invited me to see him on our next trip to Jerusalem. Exactly one year later my husband, my son and I were having breakfast with him in the Dan Pearl Hotel. An award-winning computer expert, he discussed the latest technology with Andrew, a computer programmer, and filled us in on the latest challenges facing **Common Denominator**, the organization he founded to find solutions to the disunity facing the embattled Jewish factions in Israeli society.

Peace In His Heights

Whenever Moses and the Israelites traveled, they were accompanied by the Ark. Our modern-day *Isralights*, led by Rav Binny, were never without an ancient text or a guitar to accompany us on our travels. However, on our trip to the Golan, Rav Binny also brought along his gun. Not only was he an exceptional teacher, he was also an officer in the Israeli Army who had served during the war in Lebanon. And his personal knowledge of the military battles and his poignant revelations about fellow soldiers provided an intimate dimension to his talks.

When we visited a memorial to the courageous men who died on the Golan during the Yom Kippur War, we encountered a group of young soldiers on a training expedition. Their faces carried the imprint of their ancestor's journeys to the far off lands of

Ethiopia, Russia and Morocco but now they had finally returned home. As the soldiers from around the world joined the students from around America, Rav Binny strummed his guitar and our collective voices united in divine prayer – "*. . .Osay Shalom Bimromav, Who Yasay Shalom Aleinu, V'al Kol Yisrael, Vimru, Vimru, Amen.*" (May there be abundant peace from heaven and life, upon us and upon all Israel. Now respond. Amen. *Shemoneh Esrei prayer.*)

The day concluded with a visit to the mystical city of Sefad. And it was here, in an old synagogue, that my son, Andrew, made the connection he had been searching for when Rav Binny pointed to a hole in the *Bima* and told the following story. During a street battle in the War of Independence an old man was in the midst of the Amidah prayer, *"We gratefully thank you. . ."* As he bowed down low in reverence to G-d, a piece of shrapnel that had ricocheted into the synagogue miraculously missed hitting him and lodged in the *Bima* instead.

Andrew remembered hearing this story when he was in the fourth grade. Up until now, like many of the things he had heard in the classroom, it had remained only a story. But after witnessing the actual hole in the Bima in Sefad with his own eyes, after climbing into the bombed out bunkers on the Golan and after touching the warm stones of the Kotel in Jerusalem, my father's grandson was now forever connected to the land of Israel.

This connection grew even stronger when we toured Masada several days later. While we could hear the other tour guides crunching numbers, Rav Binny focused on the human aspect of the struggle because of his own strong personal relationship with Masada. It was here that he was sworn in as a member of the Israeli Army underneath a huge sign emblazoned with the words, *"The armor is made of steel. Man is made of iron. Masada shall not fall again."*

He then quoted to us from the Book of Joshua, Chapter Eight, words that are 3200 years old and are read to every Israeli soldier; "You are passing over the Jordan this day; know that you will inherit the land."

And as each soldier individually took the oath of allegiance to the Israeli Army and the State of Israel, Rav Binny described the powerful ceremony on Masada. He related this to the time the Jewish people stood on Mt. Sinai where we collectively accepted an oath. What the Torah teaches every Jew, Rav Binny said with these stirring words, is that, *"I am an oath. I live an oath. The oath of my life is who I am and the potential of who I could be."*

It Doesn't Get Much Better Than This

After the heat and dust of Masada, Ein Gedi beckoned to us with its waterfalls and lush vegetation. While the delighted squeals of children romping in the water provided background music, Rav Binny read to us from the first book of Samuel., Chapter 23 which describes the encounter between King Saul and the young David. . . *"and he sits by the cliffs of Ein Gedi."*

"Somewhere in this path, Saul and David rediscovered their love for each other," said Rav Binny. "That's what Ein Gedi is. You're sitting in the place where David, King David Hamelech, writer of the Psalms, stood."

And as we immersed ourselves in the waters and listened to his words echo off the cliffs of Ein Gedi propelling us back to the very moment the historic encounter took place, we readily agreed with Rav Binny, "It doesn't get much better than this."

Rav Binny and his wife, Doreet, and their four children live in Efrat and that's how our *Isralight* group came to spend our second Shabbat in this town of attractive stone homes, a kind of modern day *shtetel*. After enjoying lunch with the family of Rabbi Nachum Siegel of the Happy Minyan, we strolled through the quiet streets of Efrat. As we stopped to sit on a bench under the shade of a tree that overlooked the valley, enjoying the peacefulness of that Shabbat afternoon, it was hard to believe that we were on the controversial West Bank. Another example of the paradox that is Israel.

Our group, so diverse in age and background, had become close-knit by the time we sat down for our farewell dinner together. Each of us had come to Israel searching for what was missing from our lives and as we took turns sharing the personal impressions of our journey, many of us revealed that we had found what we were looking for.

But the most profoundly moving words came from Roni, the middle-aged woman originally from Santa Barbara, California. She had grown up in a home where her father was Jewish but her mother was not. After spending her life living on the fringe she had been drawn to Israel where she retired almost ten years ago. She lived in an apartment in the old city, just steps from the Isralight Institute and although she had studied on her own and had even taken various classes over the years, this was the very first time she studied formally with a group. As a result of these special ten days she had spent with Isralight Roni shared the news that she was now prepared to undergo a traditional Orthodox conversion.

When I left Israel, I was wearing a gold ring made for me by a jeweler on Ben Yehuda Street. It is inscribed with the name of my grandmother, Chaya, my father's mother, who perished in the Holocaust. It is the name I was given at birth to honor her legacy. When I started kindergarten, Chaya was replaced by Helen, a name that was more appropriate for an American child. After searching for almost fifty years, I finally found Chaya in Jerusalem.

Epilogue:

On August 9, 2001 Rav Binny Freedman stopped into Sbarro's Restaurant on King George Street and Yaffa Road in Jerusalem for a quick bite on his way to the Isralight Institute. Suddenly, "day turned into night" as a terrorist ignited a bomb packed with nuts, bolts and screws, killing 15 people and injuring and maiming 90. Rav Binny had chosen to sit in the back of the restaurant, a decision which ultimately saved his life.

After describing the horror he had witnessed, Rav Binny concluded his powerful account of the attack with these words" "This Shabbat, in the wake of all this darkness, the Jewish people will do what we have been doing for 4,000 years; what we have always done. We will pick up the pieces and light our candles, because that is all we have ever wanted; just to bring a little light back into the world. . . May Hashem, who in His infinite Wisdom saw fit to allow me the privilege of celebrating one more Shabbat with my family, in the hills of Jerusalem, see fit to put an end to all of this pain, and all of this suffering."

Rabbi Asher Wade:
Following the Script of Life

A sher Wade is fond of quoting Shakespeare, which is not surprising for a man who was offered a teaching position at Cambridge University in England. What is astonishing is that this Chassidic Rabbi, dressed in black with a flowing gray beard, spent the first quarter century of his life also quoting the Christian gospels, chapter and verse.

As Rabbi Wade tells it, "Something happened on the way to church one morning." The spark that set off an explosive chain of events that would completely alter the life of this ordained pastor in the Methodist Church was the Commemoration of the 40th Anniversary of Kristallnacht. It was November 5, 1978 and Asher Wade, a native of Virginia, was attending the University of Hamburg in Germany working towards his doctorate in the field of metaphysics and relativity theory. He had already earned a B.A. in Philosophy in America and a post-graduate degree in philosophical theory at the University of Edinburgh, Scotland. In addition, he had previously worked as an adolescent and marriage counselor at the U.S. Army Chaplainry in Berlin while he was attending the Goethe Institute for Language Studies.

The Legacy of Kristallnacht

When Asher Wade and his German-born wife turned the pages of the local newspaper that fateful morning in November, they were shaken out of their languid Sunday routine by the graphic pictures of the destruction of the Jewish homes and stores of Hamburg during Kristallnacht. But the photograph they found most unsettling was the great synagogue of Hamburg engulfed in flames. To their horror, they immediately recognized that the site where Hamburg's once thriving 180,000 member Jewish community had worshipped was now their university's parking lot. How could this be? How could the country that had nurtured Beethoven and Goethe also be the incubator for such heinous acts of destruction?

And so their long journey began with a series of questions. "What was it like being a student on Kristallnacht? What was it like being a scholar on Kristallnacht?" And finally, "What was it like being a Christian on Kristallnact?"

When they innocently posed these three questions to the respective authorities in their community, according to Asher Wade, he and his wife were shaken out of their nest, "that comfortable position of the Cambridge elite."

As the representatives and leaders of their church, they were dismayed when they discovered that the first to join Hitler's ranks were the medical faculty, followed by the law faculty. Five out of eight students, they found out, had openly joined the Nazi party. As a result of their probing, he and his wife began to feel like "charter members of the Hamburg leper colony." They were further shocked and disillusioned with western civilization, he said, as they "stumbled across what apparently looked like the unbroken gunpowder trail from the Holocaust to the six crusades to the 305 years of the Church sanctioned Inquisition."

The Jewish Question

But now that they were out of the nest, two more positive and upbeat questions focused their attention on a new and different direction. "Who was this strange troop of people known as the Jews," they asked themselves, "who don't have a country but yet somehow or another survive with their own jurisdiction, their own laws and order, civil as well as religious, no matter where they are and no matter what language they speak."

They wanted to know, "what is this thing called Judaism?" Although he was a highly educated and knowledgeable man, Asher

Wade had never been taught a course in Judaism, and so he was determined to teach himself. Mrs. Wade, a nurse whose father and grandfather were pious Lutheran ministers, encouraged her husband to go to the source and "read the front of the bible." And once they began to compare the front of the bible, the Old Testament, with the new, they realized they had finally found the answer to their ultimate question: "What does G-d want?"

The will of our father in heaven, Asher Wade learned, was very clear. "It is to do this and not that. Eat this and not that. Behave like this and don't behave like that." They were looking for the script of life, says Rabbi Wade, and it was his wife who "got it first." It took about a year for them to reach the conclusion that Torah Judaism fulfilled all the "intellectual, academic, spiritual and emotional truths" for which they had been searching. And although he had it made in two worlds, academia and the world of religion, Reverend Wade withdrew from the church, left the ministry, converted to Judaism and he and his wife moved to the United States.

While living in America, he was contacted by Ner Israel Yeshiva in Baltimore, which led to him and his family being sent to Jerusalem, where he learned for a number of years at Ohr Somayach. Today, Rabbi and Mrs. Wade and their six children live in Jerusalem, where he lectures, counsels, teaches and conducts tours of Yad Vashem.

When audiences hear his riveting story, the question on most people's minds is, "What was your parent's reaction?" He was surprised to discover that when his mother and father were first married they lived in an Orthodox Jewish neighborhood and had Jewish friends, so they were familiar with the laws of kashruth and Shabbos. Therefore they were supportive of Asher and his wife's decision to convert and readily provided separate dishes and a separate microwave when they visited.

His in-laws, however, were initially devastated by their conversion to Judaism. However, after four solo trips to Israel, his wife's mother was so impressed by the spirituality and modesty of their lives, she convinced her husband, the minister, that "they're living the Bible. Everything we preach, they're doing."

After visiting them in Jerusalem and seeing this for himself, the minister has finally made peace with them.

What's In a Name?

Rabbi Wade revealed that he took the name Asher, spelled alef, shin, resh, which means fortunate and happy, because it described exactly how he felt about what he had found. But each time his Chassidim greeted him with Reb "*Usher*," he tried unsuccessfully to correct their pronunciation. "My name is Asher. Not Usher. It's Asher."

Then suddenly one day he realized, "*Mamish*, they're right. My name is Usher. It's *Hashgacha Protis*. They're telling me my job description. It fits me like a glove. What is an *usher* in English? That's the guy in the long black coat standing outside the revolving door of the theater of life with a script in his hands telling all the latecomers and stragglers, come on in the plot hasn't thickened yet, Moshiach hasn't arrived yet."

Rabbi Wade agrees with Shakespeare that the whole world is a stage and we are but the actors on it. However, he points out, "It's just that some of us actors got the script. And that was us *yiddin* at Har Sinai and they call it *Torat Chaim*." Asher Wade was searching for the script of life and he and his wife found it nineteen years ago and they haven't stopped following it since.

The Ultimate Makeover

osher wig? Check. High neckline? Check. Low hemline? Check. Can this observant woman standing next to her husband, Tuvia, and two sons, Ariel and Shalom, be the actress, singer and dancer formerly known as Christine Horii? Some stories are worthy of Hollywood endings. Ours has a Hollywood beginning.

Act One: A young Japanese-American leaves her home and family in Hawaii and travels to Los Angeles to fulfill her dream of stardom. She ultimately acts, sings and dances her way to Broadway appearing in such hits as *Miss Saigon* and *Shogun* and at Radio City Music Hall as one of the world famous *Rockettes.*

Act Two: Enter Todd Factor, producer, director and the love of her life. Although not religious himself, he makes it clear that marriage outside his faith is not an option. Todd is definitely leading man material, but is she ready to accept the role of a lifetime? To learn more about Judaism she heads for mecca, her local Barnes & Noble superstore. Impressed with what she reads, she begins to study in earnest.

The incredible story of how Christine Horii from Hawaii became Rachel Factor of Jerusalem is told with pathos, with humor and with affection in her one-woman show, *J.A.P.,* currently charming audiences across the U.S.A. and Canada.

When the curtain rises and we first meet Rachel, she is a lone figure dwarfed by an empty stage. But as she artfully weaves together the story of her life through words and music, this gifted performer populates the stage with a supporting cast that includes her loving family, her friends, her mentors and her rabbis.

Fateful Encounters of the Best Kind

Even though Rachel had undergone a Conservative conversion, when it came time to pick a mohel for her first-born, "I wanted the best," she confides during an interview. The best, Rabbi Paysach Krohn, gently encouraged her to reconsider an Orthodox conversion for the benefit of her children.

Fate intervened once again when the couple spent Shabbos in the home of their Queens neighbor, Rabbi Yehudah Zakutinsky, founder and director of the outreach organization, *Hashevaynu*.

"I never experienced anything like the warmth and beauty of that day," Rachel admits. "It was both Shabbos and Succos, and Adina, the rabbi's wife, had prepared a beautiful feast for the forty people invited to their sukkah."

Rabbi Zakutinsky's eloquent talk about the Jewish people spoke to them on a very personal level. The following week Simchas Torah fell on Shabbos. Inspired by what they had encountered in the Zakutinsky home, "we kept our first Shabbos and have kept every Shabbos since."

Another fateful encounter. Each Friday, Todd looked forward to the weekly visits from the young Chabadniks who came to his workplace to put on tefillin. After leaving Queens, Rachel decided a pair of tefillin would be the perfect birthday gift for her husband. The purchase brought Rabbi Simcha Kallus into their lives and so began Todd's study of Torah. Learning after work, he became so intensely involved he often didn't return home until 3 a.m. When he confessed that he was "happier than I've ever been in my life," the couple realized that this was exactly the kind of purpose-filled, spiritual life they wanted for their growing family.

For Rachel this would mean more than just a fashion overhaul. This was the ultimate makeover. "I could no longer act or dance professionally." Or so she thought, totally unaware of the significant new role that was waiting for her in the wings.

"My *parnassa* came from television and print commercials, but *tznius* (modesty) meant I had to give all of that up." Was she ready? Rachel eagerly renewed her commitment to Judaism by an Orthodox Beis Din and never looked back.

Why Rachel? "It wasn't my first choice, but the rabbis had suggested a more meaningful, traditional name like Sarah or Rachel." Initially concerned that such a name was a lot to live up to, she eventually deferred to the rabbis' wisdom. "I thought there must be a reason they are asking this of me and after I learned the history and legacy of Rachel, I'm so glad I followed their advice."

Building For The Future

With the encouragement of Rabbi Kallus they traveled to Israel, where Todd, now Tuvia planned to study for three months at Aish HaTorah in the Old City. Just three days into their trip Jerusalem had already worked its magic on them. They wanted to make Israel their permanent home.

"We thought maybe we were just being romantic and crazy so we decided to give ourselves some time," Rachel recalled. Celebrating the high holidays in Israel and spending an inspiring Shabbos with the people of Kohav Yaakov near Ramallah clinched it for them. "We would make aliyah."

When their second son, Shalom, was born, Rachel's mother made the arduous trip from Hawaii. "It was very difficult for her but she wanted to see her grandson and she, too, fell in love with Jerusalem."

The bris took place in Mea Shearim, and (gasps from the audience at this revelation) renowned Rabbi Shalom Yosef Elyashiv was the baby's *Sandak*. Rachel marvels that, "I, who had once been uncomfortable saying the word G-d, have children who say the *shema* every night at bedtime."

While Tuvia continued learning with Rabbi Moshe Greenfield at Aish HaTorah, Rachel wrote and performed a one-woman show for female audiences. When Shani, the rabbi's wife, enthusiastically endorsed Rachel's performance, the rabbi became instrumental in bringing the show to a world-wide audience. For Rachel this is the fulfillment of another dream.

"The proceeds from this tour will build a Center for the Theater Arts in Jerusalem, a special place where women can maintain their religious ideals and give to their children and their community. We have *baalei teshuvah* with amazing skills, who will use their talents to teach courses like drama, writing, fitness and dance." Rachel envisions a performance space which will include an educational children's theater for original works based on torah stories.

"With a firm belief in Hashem," she is convinced that, "after we return from our tour the arts center will happen." Like her biblical namesake who devoted her life to her children, Rachel Factor has merited that her *"efforts and endeavors will be rewarded."* (Jerimiah. 31:14)

Epilogue:

Rachel Factor built it and they came. Today, The Jerusalem Women's Center for Theater Arts, HaMachol Shel B'nos Miriam, named in honor of the woman who sang praises to G-d during the exodus from Egypt, offers classes in ballet, drama, jazz, vocal, cardio and more – all in accordance with Torah values.

Embracing the "Gifts of a Stranger"

While most us are content to live our lives with our two feet planted firmly on solid ground, terra firma isn't for everyone. Take Ahuvah Gray, for example, one of those special souls who were always destined to soar.

African-American by birth, "but Jewish by *neshama*," Ahuvah reveals that "The first thing my father asked when I told him that I was moving to Israel was where will you live and how will you support yourself when you don't even know the language?" But she was so motivated by her "spiritual yearnings to become a Jew," she just plunged right into her remarkable mission. "Now, as I look back at my decision eleven years later, I realize what a tremendous undertaking it was at the time."

It comes as no surprise, therefore, that *Lech Lecha* (Genesis 12:1), the biblical account of a man who voluntarily uproots himself, leaving his family, his home and everything familiar, to embark on a spiritual journey fraught with hardship and danger, is Ahuvah Gray's favorite *parsha*. The story of her personal Lech Lecha is described in detail in her autobiography, **My Sister, The Jew**. Ahuvah's extraordinary journey continues in her sequel, **Gifts of a Stranger**, recently published by Targum/Feldheim.

Born and raised in Chicago, Ahuvah began her travels at an early age, when she and her siblings returned each summer to the rural south of Mound Bayou, Mississippi, where she learned to love the Psalms in the nurturing home of her maternal grandparents. Influenced by her grandmother's strong commitment to prayer, Ahuvah notes that, *"Tehillim* have always been an inspiration in my life," and she is convinced that "it is in the *zechus,* the merit of my grandmother, that I have made this journey."

But Ahuvah Gray's journey from an airline stewardess for Continental to a rising star in corporate America and then the owner of her own travel business which took her to Israel fourteen times, did not end with her Aliyah and conversion to Orthodox Judaism. Ahuvah is once again navigating the globe, but this time her route is determined by Jewish geography. A skilled communicator, she's already amassed an impressive itinerary, touching down and touching audiences from Australia to Hong Kong as she shares the gifts of her spirituality.

But it was in her own backyard that a chance meeting with a troubled young woman, who felt oppressed by the burden of her religion, was destined to change both of their lives. Shira Taylor of Capetown, South Africa was sitting in the audience the day that Ahuvah Gray was invited to lecture at the Aish Hatorah Fellowships program in Jerusalem. Overwhelmed with emotion by Ahuvah's deeply moving personal story, Shira later wrote, "From about the age of eighteen I had unconcernedly watched as my Judaism gradually dwindled to a shadow of what it had once been. I stopped keeping kosher and learned absolutely no Torah. . .I, who had been handed the Torah on a silver platter with an excellent Jewish education, a family immersed in Torah life and parents who were so trusting, patient and giving. I wept for the lost years where I had been frozen and closed and ignorant. I wept because Ahuvah had fought so hard and with such love and joy for what I had always dismissed."

Ahuvah attributes Shira's miraculous change in attitude to Divine Providence. *"Hashem* made me the messenger that brought about Shira Taylor's spiritual reawakening," she writes in **Gifts of a Stranger,** "and in doing so we both created a fundamental shift in the world. Her world changed dramatically. My world expanded and was enriched, her story continues to inspire other people and the chain of responsibility goes on."

It is this sincere sense of responsibility that compels Ahuvah to eagerly share her story. She feels humbled by her unique ability to provide fellow Jews with *chizuk,* but at the same time she's not bashful about suggesting that converts have "the spiritual genes of Avraham *Avinu,* the first *Ger."*

Admitting that she used to say "I was always a woman of great *emunah,* but when you become a Jew you have to become a person of great patience," she marvels at the personal and professional choices she made throughout her life which ultimately led to her conversion. "Hashem does things in their time. There are no coincidences with Hashem. . .everything that happens comes from Hashem."

A natural teacher, Ahuvah draws on both of her cultural heritages combining her lyrical African-American cadences with the richness of biblical imagery and the result is magical. When you look into the spellbound faces of seminary students, you immediately sense that they find her story especially meaningful.

During a recent lecture tour across America, Ahuvah found that her deep love for the power and meaning of prayer resonated very strongly with these young women who ultimately seek her out when they come to Israel. "Seminary girls from around the world have been to my home for Shabbos meals."

Home is the loving community of *Bayit Vegan.* House and garden, even the name conjures up an idealized vision of white picket fences. But Ahuvah's abode, not surprisingly, is perched high above the streets, closer to the heavens. From an aerie with a commanding view of the adopted country she loves, Ahuvah Gray reaches out to the world and invites us to continue the journey with her as she ascends to new heights.

beginners in Crown Heights. First she learned the *Modeh Ani* prayer, then the food *brachas*. And for the first time in her life, at 57 years of age, Lieba Marcia Schwartz heard the sound of the shofar.

"You can leave Judaism, but Judaism can never leave you because G-d gave you a little spark of himself, a *neshama*," she told a roomful of women during an evening sponsored by Mayon Chai, *The Center for Inspiration and Chizuck*. To this largely 'frum from birth' crowd in Boro Park Lieba confided, "I'm also an FFB, *farblongit from birth*."

"We are lost, but we are not a lost cause," she assured them. And although she has shared her miraculous story with audiences throughout America, she welcomed the opportunity to speak before this particular group of women so she could finally say, "Thank you."

"You have continued to light your Shabbos candles and lead a Jewish life so that I had somewhere to come home to. And when you light a candle," she reminded them, "you are lighting a candle in the heart of some Jewish woman who is not doing it yet."

Lieba encouraged the women, who were visibly moved by her gratitude, not to underestimate the power of what just one woman can do. "One woman turned my life upside down and right side up with just two words, *Good Shabbos*."

Integrating Torah With Technology: A Success Story

M om, am I Jewish?"
"Yes, by birth. But we don't believe in that."

Akiva Shapiro chuckles as he remembers this conversation with his mother that took place over a decade ago. The remarkable saga of his transformation from a Wall Street computer mogul, totally ignorant about Judaism, to a man who has created a life and a company built on Torah values has all the ingredients of a classic epic.

In The Beginning

Although Akiva's grandparents were Reform, his father became a *baal teshuvah* as a teenager. But he mysteriously lost his faith and ultimately changed his name from Shapiro to Shepherd to avoid being identified as a Jew. His mother, a fifth generation American, was a member of the Ethical Culture Society that believed since goodness is innate in human beings we'll keep the ethics but delete the rituals and the concept of God from our lives. When their son was born they named him Kenneth Shepherd Jr. and raised him without any connection to his heritage.

"I didn't know what the Torah was and never even heard of Yom Kippur," he admits.

His father's untimely death, when Akiva was six, and his mother's subsequent remarriage and divorce, threw the once straight A student into such turmoil he almost dropped out of high school. Although his mother was always supportive and stood by him throughout his troubled youth, at the age of 19 he decided it was time to set out on his own. He camped across the country ending up in Hollywood where he took acting courses, waited on tables and got a license driving 18-wheelers. He was also on a spiritual quest, investigating everything from Buddhism to Christianity, but found too much "production" and very little substance.

The Rise

A subsequent cross-country trip ended when his vehicle was destroyed in a snowstorm. "So what do you do when you're faced with no money and no job – you join the army." Stationed for a year and a half in Frankfurt Germany, he is grateful to the military for providing him with something he never had, discipline, which served him extremely well. He also became a voracious reader, discovering that he loved to learn, so that after returning home he enrolled in Westchester Community College and explored every facet of college life.

Searching for his niche he became a DJ and wrote for the college newspaper, but it was a computer class in Fortran that proved to be his wakeup call. "I knew right away this was exactly what I wanted to do with my life."

High grades brought him a scholarship to Iona College where he received a B.A. in computer science, graduating Summa Cum Laude with a 4.0 index. During this time his marriage to a Catholic girl ended after a year and a half when they both realized they had made a mistake.

While still in college, an internship at IBM Management Development Sector exposed Akiva to the most advanced management techniques in the world, where they trained their first line, middle line, senior and executive managers. It was an invaluable education that ultimately became the cornerstone of his career. Upon graduation, GE was so impressed with his academic achievements they offered him a position in an elite program normally reserved for Ivy League graduates.

In 1989 he established his own software development business, Cutting Edge Computer Consulting that later became

Framework Inc. By 1994 he and an associate had built the company into over a million dollars in revenue, when he sold the majority of shares to pursue other interests. A fortuitous consulting job with Bankers Trust, where he saved them "a lot of money," landed him a job as Vice President in charge of Software Development. The huge career jump provided him with a sizable income that allowed him to indulge in an $800,000 lavishly furnished apartment with two balconies overlooking Manhattan, a full-time cook and a Mercedes motorcycle.

And Fall

"I thought I was golden on Wall Street, making a lot of money doing what I loved, when suddenly my hopes for the future collapsed."

Just as he was positioning Bankers Trust for development into the 21st century, Deutsche Bank took over and he found himself out of work. More *tsuris*. His childless second marriage, this time to a Jewish girl, ended after 6 years.

"I was 35 years old with no job, no money, no home, no kids, no family and no happiness." Forced to assess his life he wondered one night, does God exist? "So I decided I'm gonna make a prayer to God. I said, God if you exist, just help me believe. That was my whole prayer."

Once he opened himself up, things started to happen immediately. When an acquaintance suggested to him that 'Shapiro' was a nice name and it was a shame his family had changed it to Shepherd, for the first time in his life he felt a sense of pride in the name Shapiro."

Contemplating this conversation as he stood on the corner of 57th and Lexington in Manhattan, Akiva experienced an "aha!" moment. Holding a Starbucks coffee in one hand and a cigarette in the other, "it was suddenly crystal clear that I needed to become a good Jew in order to bring Judaism back into my lineage and redeem the soul of my father. I didn't know what a 'good Jew' was at the time. I thought maybe good Jew meant to change my name back to Shapiro and send my kids to Hebrew school."

Enter Rebbetzin Esther Jungreis. He had recently heard

about her outreach organization, *Hineni,* and decided that was his next stop, but he was unprepared for the sight that greeted him the following Tuesday night when he walked into a room packed with 2,000 young secular Jews. "As I pushed open the door I heard this woman's voice say, 'If you don't believe in God, make a prayer to God. God will help you believe.' Okay you've got my attention, I thought. Halfway through the class she hits me with the zinger. 'If your father turned away from God you can redeem the soul of your father because a tree is measured by the quality of its fruit.'

"That was it. Tears were streaming down my face. I was sobbing. I had gone from a prayer to a spiritual experience to a physical confirmation of that spiritual experience in less than a week."

By the end of the evening he was convinced the rebbetzin was going to make a difference in his life. He introduced himself and "she started meeting with me weekly and ultimately became a very important mentor to me."

Another meaningful encounter. At Hineni he met Yisroel Neuberger, author of *From Central Park to Sinai,* who was also a *baal teshuvah* from the Ethical Culture Society. "He totally related to me and knew exactly where I was coming from."

Invited to his shul on Shabbos, Akiva surveyed the sea of black hats and thought, "Oh my goodness, I've entered Mormon country. Getting up and down and speaking in a language I didn't understand, I thought this is the weirdest thing." But later at the Neuberger home "there was the Shabbos table and there was singing and love and family and simcha. I looked at this with tears in my eyes and thought this is exactly what I've been picturing since I was 24 years old and decided I wanted a family."

And Rise

Akiva stayed up all that night watching TV, flipping through the channels, when he realized "every single thing I was watching was meaningless. My whole life is meaningless, my past is meaningless, my job is meaningless, and my marriage was meaningless. Everything I've done has been selfish and meaningless, but what I just experienced this weekend was reality.

I turned off the TV and went to sleep determined to be *Shomer Shabbos* from that moment on." Koshering his home, wearing *tsitsit* and putting on *tefillin* were soon to follow.

Next came a weekend with Gateways Seminar, where he was told "you could grab a rabbi and speak to him all night long." And so he did. "Rabbi Moshe Lichtenstein, who heads Project Gesher, became my mentor and my rebbe who has helped me at the *Halachic* level and spiritual level. He and Rebbetzin Jungreis have been the two most influential people in my life."

When the Rebbetzin told Akiva that **Hineni** needed a computer-dating program he had one ready. For some unexplainable reason he had already written such a program during the time he was out of work even though he had no idea what he was going to do with it. The program indirectly led him to his future wife.

Chani had come to Hineni after reading *The Committed Life*. She was so moved by the story of the rebbetzin's grandfather, who reminded her so much of her own grandfather, "I just wanted to tell her how much of an impact the story made on me."

Rebbetzin Jungreis had her own agenda. Immediately upon meeting Chani she said, "I have a *shidduch* for you." She introduced her to Akiva, who was busy running the computer Shidduch program. They were engaged after five dates and married shortly afterward.

"I didn't know what *nachas* meant until I saw this little baby," Akiva says lovingly of his daughter, Yehudis. He finally has the family life he always dreamed of and now he also has 35 *mishpachas* counting on him. When he decided to create another company, he sought to incorporate torah and *kiruv* with technology. The result was GSI, a software development company which trains *frum* unemployed computer programmers in IBM technology.

Akiva is proud that GSI has over 35 IBM certifications with an unbelievable team of people. According to Gershon Orenstein who has 22 years experience in the mainframe world, 18 years as a programmer/analyst, 4 years as a project manager, "There is a tremendous need to help people find *parnassa* in a kosher environment. This model of a frum environment coupled with the highest standards of professionalism and the latest state-of-the-art technology is an unbeatable combination and very much needed to help Yeshiva, Kollel and Seminary grads transition to the real world."

Programmer Yitzchok Loriner echoes these sentiments. "Another reason for the success of the company is the strong focus that Akiva places on the company being a place of spiritual growth as well as technical and financial." All work stops at 1:30 p.m. when the men learn and women say tehillim. Says Dovid Weiss, "an hour every day dedicated to Torah learning followed by *mincha* adds a spiritual component that gives the entire workday a different meaning."

Surveying the miracles in his life, Akiva Shapiro is proud that he has "built a company on Torah values that can bring *parnassa* to *frum* Jews.

"It is incumbent on me as a *Baal Teshuvah* to give everything back to Hashem who has given me so much," says Akiva. "We're on the verge of success and it's perfectly clear to me that everything will happen according to his will."

A Wedding In Montreal

*O*ui. *Oui. Trés bien. Au revoir."*

After holding an animated conversation on his cell phone, in perfect French, the young man scanned the menu and turned to his companion and asked, *"Vuz loz mir essen?"* (What should we eat?) in perfect Yiddish.

I observed this scene with a mixture of amusement and admiration from an adjacent table in the Chabad Cafe in downtown Montreal, fascinated by yet another example of the adaptability of the wandering Jew. No matter what foreign soil the body may be transplanted to, the Yiddishe *neshama* always manages to stay connected to its roots.

All In The Family

My own personal history has left me acutely aware of this never-ending cycle of connecting and reconnecting which is the defining experience of our exile. After the Holocaust, my family immigrated to America, while my father's sole surviving relative, cousin Herschel Rudski, settled in Canada with his wife and two sons. Both parents had to work and so they enrolled the boys in a Lubavitch yeshiva. They were not religious, just concerned that their children should be safe and well looked after during their long workday. While the older son, Sam, attended for a short period of time, his younger brother Ephraim remained a student throughout his formative years.

Hershel was actually my father's second cousin, an

insignificant relation in most other families, but because we had no other family on my father's side and were bereft of any cousins, his occasional visits to Brooklyn became a much anticipated part of my childhood. I remember cousin Hershel as a man with a gentle demeanor who was always happy in my father's presence. The two men would sit for hours and reminisce about another time and place, reconnecting to a world they could never share with us.

When Hershel's son, Ephraim, became a teenager, he frequently stopped at our home during his travels to Brooklyn, wearing a neatly pressed white shirt and black yarmulke, which stood out in stark contrast to the casual, colorful attire of the hippie era. My parents explained that he had become a *Lubavitcher* and his ultimate destination was a *farbrengen* with the Rebbe in Crown Heights. Brighton Beach was not a hotbed of Chassidism in the 1960s so it was not until several decades later, when my own spiritual journey ultimately led me to 770 and a blessing from the Rebbe, that I came to understand the meaning of the mysterious term "Lubavitcher."

During the intervening years, as we busied ourselves with college, careers and finally families of our own, babies were born and a whole new generation grew up who remained strangers to their relatives across the border. And then when Hershel and my father were no longer with us, the fragile family connection seemed finally severed.

Connections & Reconnections

Now my cousin is a grandfather with a long graying beard and I have come to Montreal in the summer of 2000 with my husband and daughter, Sara, to participate in the marriage celebration of one of his ten children. As I stand outside the banquet hall and watch the wedding scene unfolding in the street below, I review the sequence of miraculous events that have ultimately brought us to this time and place. But the random coincidences and complex plot twists further reinforce my belief that only fate could have reconnected our family with Ephraim, his brother, Sam, and their wives and children.

A recent phone call from my friend, Elise Lantor, once again reminded me how these fateful connections and reconnections intricately weave themselves into the fabric of our lives. Her daughter Danielle, who was studying in Jerusalem, was invited by a friend to meet a newly married couple from Montreal, who had just moved to Israel. After Danielle filled the couple in on the details of how she became observant through her connection with Lubavitch and Rebbetzin Esther Winner, the young bride asked, "If you know Esther Winner, then maybe you know my cousin because they made a video together. Her name is Helen Schwimmer."

When I Came Home, I Really Came Home

This is the stuff made-for-T.V. movies are made of. Our heroes, a couple of starry-eyed, secular Jewish teens, meet up at a Grateful Dead concert. Known as Dead-Heads, Sara and Butterfly travel together, following the popular rock group around the country. When their journey ultimately becomes a quest for spirituality, the teens part ways as Butterfly embraces Judaism while Sara becomes enamored of a cult in Vermont.

Fearing she is being held captive, Sara's parents enlist Butterfly's help in a heroic effort to rescue their daughter. After an exhausting seven-hour trip and a harrowing middle-of-the-night confrontation with the cult, Butterfly finally convinces his friend to leave the group and they tearfully ride off into the night together.

Today, Butterfly, Dov Yonah Korn, lives with his wife, Sara, and their two children in lower Manhattan where they are deeply involved in the outreach activities of Chabad of Greenwich Village. This earnest young man shared the spellbinding details of his transformation from a follower of the Grateful Dead to a follower of the Lubavitcher Rebbe, as we sat warmed by a blazing campfire, under a magical country sky.

I have come to learn at **Machon Chana in the Mountains** during the summer of 2001. Located on the grounds of the former Diamond Horseshoe Ranch and Resort in Tannersville, New York, the property, where horses once roamed, has been converted into an idyllic site where Torah is now studied. It is here, in the shadow of Kaaterskill Falls, that women, men and students of all ages and backgrounds have come to deepen their connection to their heritage, choosing from a smorgasbord of summer programs. Everyone has a unique story to share and they are as inspiring as the classes.

When Joan Hutchinson of San Antonio, Texas began to experience a religious awakening, she first headed for the neighborhood Conservative synagogue. As she sat alone in the room that was three quarters empty, she was disappointed that "no one even came over to say hello." Determined to find her Jewish niche, Joan next turned to the local Chabad House.

Her voice fills with emotion as she recounts her initial response. "I was overwhelmed with the feeling that when I came home, I really came home," said Joan. "Everyone welcomed me with open arms."

Her trip to Machon Chana is indicative of her resolve to literally travel to great lengths to immerse herself in Jewish teachings. From San Antonio Joan first flew into Houston and then on to St. Louis. Next came a stopover in Baltimore and then finally, after landing in Albany, she rented a car and drove to Tannersville. After hearing about her arduous trip, my three-hour sojourn from Brooklyn no longer seemed like such a *schlep!*

While most people move from the north to the south, Lynne Russell's journey took her in the opposite direction. As she and her daughter became more observant, they realized that they would have to look for a school outside of their town of Fort Myers, Florida. The yeshiva that appealed to her daughter was located in Boro Park, Brooklyn and that's where Lynne, now Leah, and her daughter happily reside. Machon Chana, which offered classes as varied as the *Fundamentals of Jewish Belief, Rashi Analysis* and *Challah Baking,* was the next stop on Leah's itinerary.

Aviva Spiegel, who left a budding career in research at Stanford University, discovered herself and her *bashert* in Jerusalem. Presently, she lives with her husband and two children in Flatbush, Brooklyn. A former gymnast, Aviva teaches classes in creative movement, encouraging us to tap into the child with each of us.

Children could be seen and heard everywhere at Machon

Chana. It was refreshing to sit and listen to Rabbi Eli Silberstein teach a *Chumash* class, while a toddler sat contentedly on his lap. Or to hear Rabbi Chaim Adelman give a *derusha* with his infant perched on his shoulder. For the young women enrolled in the LIFT program (Living Inspiration for Teens), whose accents revealed Russian, English and Middle Eastern backgrounds, it was a lesson in integrating the teachings of Judaism into their daily lives.

And for late-bloomers like myself, **Machon Chana in the Mountains** was another defining stop along the route to my roots. And in spite of occasional frustrations with my lack of knowledge and textural skills, remarkable people and meaningful experiences continue to accompany me on this sacred journey, proving that getting there is half the fun.

IX

Israel, M.A.T.C.K.H. and 9/11

*A*s the horrific images of the latest intifada were splashed across the television and computer screens, I watched with mounting horror as the people of Israel were being brutally attacked, both physically and in the mainstream media. I composed letters and sent emails. I made monetary contributions to organizations aiding victims of terror. By January 2001 I could no longer sit idly by and watch the Jewish nation increasingly shunned and isolated and decided to travel to Israel on my own personal solidarity mission.

I stayed in the hotels and ate in restaurants. I prayed at the deserted kotel where there were often more soldiers than worshippers. I went to Israel because it wasn't enough just to send money for ambulances or bullet proof vests or children who had lost their arms and legs and parents. I needed to walk the streets of Jerusalem once again and I needed to learn. I enrolled in Shearim, a women's college in Har Nof where I studied with excellent teachers like founder and director, Rebbetzin Holly Pavlov.

When I returned to America, I received a call from Molly Resnick, a veteran journalist with NBC who is the founder and director of M.A.T.C.K.H., *Mothers Against Teaching Children to Kill and Hate.* Since 1998 the organization has developed educational programs to inform the public and lobby officials to oppose groups teaching bigotry, hatred and murder to children.

MATCKH understood that when leaders stood on the White House lawn and amicably shook hands while children throughout the Middle East were simultaneously being taught daily by their parents, by their teachers and by their government to kill Jews and Americans, it was an empty gesture. Molly Resnick was one of the first to sound the alarm that fanatical Muslims were indoctrinating children and raising a generation of suicide bombers. Unless the hate-filled curriculum was changed, Molly warned audiences throughout the United States, these fanatics would eventually export their terrorism.

To counter the destructive effects of this type of curriculum, MATCKH mobilized children across the country to get involved with the **"Kids For Peace"** quilt project. By writing letters to Arab children, which were to be gathered together to form a giant good-will message, children would become the messengers of peace.

I joined MATCKH and we wrote and produced **"Creating Peace One Quilt At A Time."** The documentary was endorsed by the Greater New York Board of Jewish Education, who mailed copies of the video to all of its member schools with instructions for each school to create its own peace quilt.

Under the auspices of several congressmen, MATCKH planned to bus schoolchildren and their quilts to Washington, D.C. for a massive "Kids For Peace Rally." Scheduled for October 4th, our rally never took place because Molly Resnick's prophetic warnings came true on September 11, 2001.

Terror On the 44th Floor

When you're running for your life, you can't let flimsy designer heels stand in your way, thought Agnes Ford, hurrying past several pairs of abandoned shoes as she descended the stairwell of Tower Two of the World Trade Center, escaping a terrorist attack for the second time in her life.

Tuesday, September 11th had begun like a typical work day for the Vice President in charge of contracts at Guy Carpenter Reinsurance Brokers, which occupied floors 49-54 of Tower Two. Entering the building at 8:30 a.m., Agnes headed for the bank of elevators.

"There are normally four elevators which service my area, but only two were working. Since the other two were under maintenance, there was a long wait as my other co-workers continued to arrive. We took the elevator to the 44th floor, where I then normally switch for the one that takes me to my office on the 51st floor." That's when normal life ended for Agnes Ford.

"As I stepped out of the elevator on the 44th floor, I saw debris flying past the window." Simultaneously, when the doors to the elevator coming from the upper floors opened, people poured out and headed for the stairwell. "We don't know what's going on, but we're getting out of here," they shouted. "Don't go down the elevator. Use the stairs."

Although eight years had passed, in that terrifying moment Agnes suddenly felt as if she was experiencing an instant replay of the 1993 attack on the WTC. So while her colleagues hesitated, she knew she had to get out of the building and immediately headed for the stairwell. The others followed.

As the most decisive and the tallest, Agnes found herself the leader once again, cautioning members of her group not to panic or try to push ahead. They followed her down, not knowing that the debris they had just seen was caused by a plane ramming into Tower One.

"In '93 we walked down in total darkness and silence, but this time everything worked. The stairwells were well lit and we heard continuous announcements over the public address system directing us to proceed to the street."

When they got to the fifth floor, "the building suddenly moved." The second plane had just exploded into Tower Two. Gripped with fear, their pace quickened and they reached street level within minutes, still totally unaware of what had happened to their building.

Born and bred in Brooklyn, the familiar terrain of the city suddenly turned treacherous as Agnes began to navigate the streets in an attempt to get home. Headed in the direction of the Brooklyn Bridge, she became the victim of a hit and run as a bicycle knocked her over then continued to race down the street. Bruised, she made her way toward the bridge only to find it engulfed in smoke. As she turned back, she stared in disbelief as she saw Tower Two crumble. "We thought it was built to withstand anything. This was not supposed to happen."

From the radios on the street blaring the news reports she finally learned the extent of the catastrophe. Then, passing an appliance store, she stopped to watch the horrific scenes on the television sets in the store window. As she continued northward, she met a group at 23rd street and Fifth Avenue who worked in Building Seven, a 43-story complex, who had watched in shock as the planes hit the twin towers. They also described seeing people jumping out of the buildings. "Whenever we heard planes overhead we got very nervous, because we didn't know whose planes they were."

When Agnes heard that the A and F trains were still operating, she headed for 34th Street and Sixth Avenue. The conversations she heard on the street called for retaliation. "Not out of revenge," she emphasized, "but to show that we're strong and that you can't attack the United States of America." The general feeling was that if Osama bin Laden was responsible, "we have to get him and we can't let this drag on like the '93 bombing trial."

Once safely home Agnes reflected on an ominous conversation she had with me just three days earlier. As the Special Events Coordinator for MATCKH, Mothers Against Teaching Children To Kill & Hate, I had contacted her about participating in our October 4th **"Kids For Peace"** rally in Washington, D.C. I shared with Agnes, a fellow Brooklyn College alum, my fear that the suicide bombers who were terrorizing the Middle East ultimately put the entire world in jeopardy. It was only a matter of time, I warned, before they exported their hatred and started blowing themselves up in our country. For Agnes Ford and America, the unthinkable had become a reality.

Epilogue:

Among the 298 people killed at the World Trade Center who worked with Agnes was the company nurse, Lydia, who was looking forward to her wedding day.

The other surviving employees of Marsh McLennan-Guy Carpenter Reinsurance brokers have been scattered throughout the tristate area. In each of the New York, New Jersey and Connecticut locations a memorial has been erected to honor the dead with the names of the victims inscribed in stone and lucite. No mention is made of how they died or who killed them.

Rabbi, Wife, Twins Miraculously Survive WTC Attack To Light Menorah of Hope

It's a miracle that Rabbi Shmaya Katz is lighting a menorah opposite Ground Zero each night this week, because on September 11th he was afraid he might not live to see another Chanukah.

The Director of Chabad of Wall Street had just left his apartment in Battery Park City, when suddenly he heard a terrifying blast and the sky literally seemed to be falling. As people in the streets ran screaming in all directions the young rabbi's first thought was that "*Moshiach* had come or, G-d forbid, the opposite," so he rushed back to his pregnant wife and their two year-old twins. "We have to evacuate," he shouted running into their second floor apartment located a block and a half from the World Trade Center.

Just minutes before, Rochel Katz had peered outside her window at the clear blue sky. It's a perfect day for an outing for her young boys, Avraham and Moshe Yitzrak, she thought, when suddenly she was shocked to see a plane appear overhead. Then came a horrendous sound she will never forget. As she felt the earth shake she was sure the plane had crashed into her building.

The Rabbi and his wife each grabbed a child and headed for their mini-van that was parked a block away. "We thought the bridges were open and we could drive to Brooklyn." But as they ran toward the van, they were overwhelmed by fear as fragments of steel rained down on them and the air became so thick with white ash they felt *"it was worse than the plague of darkness in Egypt and a blind person could see more than us."*

Their only hope was a faint light in the distance so the rabbi guided his wife toward the glow as they began choking from the ash that was filling their throats.

Clutching her child tightly to protect him from the debris assaulting his body, Rochel Katz was convinced she saw the Angel of Death appear before her. With the little breath that they had left the rabbi and his wife each said *"Shema,"* and pleaded for G-d to forgive them for their sins and "open up Gan Eden for us." Darkness and an eerie silence enveloped them as they continued to stumble helplessly toward the light.

Miraculously, a building suddenly appeared before them and the door swung open as helpful hands pulled them safely inside.

"When the doctor examined, us he said we were lucky we weren't brain damaged from the lack of oxygen," said Rochel. The children are still traumatized. They draw pictures and tell me "this is the *bomb day,* mommy."

Cookies Fresh From The Ohel

Most of the time a cookie is just a cookie, except when it becomes a mitzvah. This one first took shape on Lag B'Omer, the *yahrzeit* of Rabbi Shimon bar Yochai, the author of the Kabbalistic work, the *Zohar*, which delves into the mystical aspects of the Torah.

It's a tradition to pray at the Ohel, the gravesite of the Lubavitcher Rebbe, to commemorate this auspicious day, so when I arrived at the Old Montefiore Cemetery in Queens, I wasn't surprised to be greeted by several good friends, until I discovered that they were also there for my surprise Hebrew birthday party arranged by my rebbetzin, Esther Winner.

Before I even knew I had a Hebrew birthday or that it coincided with a holiday called Lag B'Omer, I was inexplicably drawn to the study of Kabbalah and purchased my own Zohar. Years later, when Jewish mysticism became trendy, red-stringed kabbalah bracelets were flying off the virtual shelves of my daughter Sara's online Judaica store, Chosencouture.com.

On this particularly mystical May afternoon, my friends chose to gather together in the giant outdoor tent, erected next to the Ohel, and celebrate with a home-made lunch which included the most delicious chocolate chip cookies baked by my friend, master chef Levana Kirschenbaum. Her family had founded the first gourmet kosher restaurant in Manhattan, appropriately named, Levana. I met and worked with her when she launched another innovation, the first gourmet kosher cooking school in

New York City, *Levana's Place at Lincoln Square Synagogue.*

Whenever she came to pray at the Ohel, Levana asked what she could do to help our beleaguered brethren in Israel. Do what comes naturally, came the answer this time. Bake cookies. When Levana revealed that her dream was to bake one million cookies to raise funds for the families of the victims of terror I knew there was one person who could help her make it a reality, Neil Thalheim, the founder and director of the Israel Emergency Solidarity Fund. He did. And the **Million Cookies Project** was born.

A place to bake? Piece of cake. The Upper West Side Jewish Community Center donated their modern new kitchen and an army of volunteers, which included doctors, social workers, artists, and lawyers, working alongside moms, students and retirees pitched in to help Levana reach her goal of baking and selling one million cookies by the end of summer. This monster-sized order might have scared an ordinary mortal, but for Levana, who first began her career with a specialty bakery, raising dough came naturally. And she took the command, *"Don't slumber and don't sleep, watch over Israel"* (Psalm 121), very seriously by baking her gourmet chocolate chip cookies from 9 am till 9 pm four days a week.

In honor of Rosh Chodesh Elul (August 2002), just three months after the Million Cookie Project was first conceived, thousands of visitors to the Ohel were treated to the cookies baked with love for Israel. The sponsor was my husband, who also wanted to take an active role in this meaningful mitzvah. And for Levana Kirschenbaum, who finally fulfilled her dream of helping the people of Israel, the project was doubly sweet because Lag B'Omer is also the yahrzeit of her dear father.

X

The Refugee Boat and the Luxury Liner

For Jews, travel has always been more than just an excuse to visit the trendiest new vacation spot or to hike up a mountain to be wowed by the view. There's always a moral to our story as well as our trip.

My life as a wandering Jew began the day my parents packed up their meager possessions, three cardboard boxes tied with rope, along with my nine month old brother and joined over 1,200 other displaced persons aboard the General Harry Taylor. Named for the Chief of Engineers who had received the Distinguished Service Medal during World War I, the General Taylor was a converted military transport that had once carried troops and supplies to battle in the Pacific. Now its cargo consisted of the surviving remnant of a generation.

On the sixth day after we left the German port of Bremenhafen, the sea became treacherous. When it looked as if we were in danger of sinking, an SOS was sent out and the Queen Elizabeth, the closest ship cruising in the vicinity, came to our rescue. For twenty-four hours the luxury liner and the refugee boat traveled side by side until the waters became calm. My maiden voyage across the Atlantic ended on January

184 / "LIKE THE STARS OF THE HEAVENS"

22, 1951 when the General Taylor docked at our new address, the United States of America. I was three and a half years old.

HIAS (Hebrew Immigrant Aid Society) housed us temporarily in a 26 story building in lower Manhattan that had seen better days. Built in 1899 by August Belmont, Jr. of horse racing fame, 15 Park Row was at one time renowned as the tallest building in New York. But like the immigrants it once sheltered, the building ultimately prevailed and has risen to new heights, recently designated a New York City landmark. Today, luxury apartments occupy the upper floors while the street level is home to another landmark, J & R Music World.

This Is Not Your Mother's Borsht Belt

M incha!"
As I stood on the main street in Woodbourne, New York, I watched the man dressed in black poke his head into the doorways of the storefronts lining this sleepy little Catskill town, reminding the displaced city folk that it was time for afternoon *davening*.

Bungalow colony life is not a part of my heritage. Ever since I was a young child our family always lived on the periphery of the ocean, where the beach, and not the mountains, beckoned to us in summer. Over the years, as I watched entire families make the seasonal pilgrimage to the country, I became accustomed to seeing various Brooklyn neighborhoods take on a ghost-town appearance. This year, however, when friends who owned a home in the mountains told us of a house that was available in their community, it seemed like the ideal opportunity to finally experience this modern-day exodus for ourselves.

And so while the summer *Parsha* readings were preoccupied with the Israelites' forty-year trek through *bamidbar* (the desert), we mirrored their journey as we loaded up our caravan with the necessary rudiments of civilization and followed Route 17 west toward the promised land of fresh air and tranquility. Navigating the country roads, I finally understood how our biblical legacy has empowered generations of Jews throughout the millennia to pack up and move en masse to confront the challenges of distant countries and alien civilizations.

Country 101

Our summer in the Catskills began with a series of unforeseen challenges that made us feel like aliens in our own house. First there were the roots that we discovered had grown into the pipes in our septic tank which caused havoc with our plumbing. Then we were treated to a mid-day visit by a giant black bear that used our backyard for a shortcut into the woods. More visitors. Strange noises in our attic signaled the arrival of squirrels who became unwelcome boarders at all hours of the day and night. And, finally, we were forced to add large plastic buckets to the decor of our charming country bedroom when repeated thunderstorms sent rain cascading down our ceiling.

If sparring with Mother Nature made me question the wisdom of sampling country life, my sojourn in the Catskills convinced me that we had stumbled upon the ultimate Jewish melting pot. Back in the city, each group laid claim to their own turf, ensconced in their individual neighborhoods. Up here every group has its own enclave too; however, the absence of local shopping compels members of the different communities to converge on the retail giants. And so Wal-Mart serves as a kind of Mecca for residents of Williamsburg, Boro Park, Crown Heights, Flatbush and the Upper West Side, encouraging Jews sporting every type of head covering, skirt length and stocking configuration to mingle amicably among the *shmattes* and the potted plants. We even encountered one of my husband's patients who remarked, "I knew I could find anything I needed in Wal-Mart, but I never expected to find my pediatrician."

I witnessed another version of this convivial atmosphere in the Heimishe Oneg Bakery in Monticello. Nothing had prepared me for the sights and smells that greeted me when I walked through the door of this unassuming, rustic-looking structure. Challahs of enormous proportions, rugelach of every filling, cakes of every variety rained down like *manna* from heaven, overflowing on the store's shelves and bins and showcases. But the variety of baked goods competed with the diversity of the customers as a white-shirted *bocher* stood next to a bare-headed man in shorts, a bubby wearing a *shetel* and a chic young mother in a baseball cap, all waiting patiently in line for their Shabbos orders.

Our Catskill sabbatical coincided with the period of the three weeks before *Tisha B'av* and so I had the opportunity to visit the Homowack Hotel for the first time, when we attended a performance by the accapella singing group Beat-Achon. The stereotyped jokes I had heard comics repeat for decades about the Borsht Belt were swept away by the sacred melodies created by these earnest young men. It was hard to believe there was no music accompanying these spirited singers who represented various professions, including computer experts, lawyers and artists whose love of singing brought them together to share beautiful harmonies.

Everywhere we went we experienced this renewed sense of Jewish brotherhood. One dark night our friends, the country *mavens,* stopped their van to pick up a group of hitchhikers who from their dress were obviously Jewish. They had no qualms about getting into our van because we, too, were obviously Jewish, with slight variations in outward appearance. It was only upon stepping inside that one of the young men dressed in black was pleasantly surprised to find himself looking into the smiling face of his pediatrician, my husband.

Chazak

I was delighted to discover that The Jewish Renaissance Center, whose thought-provoking, inspiring classes for women I had attended in Manhattan, was relocating upstate for three days. The beautiful grounds of Luxor Estates in Loch Sheldrake hosted over 300 women who had come from all over the Catskills to listen to Rabbi Moshe Weinberger, Rabbi Jonathan Rietti and Director, Mrs. Leah Kohn, discuss the writings of *Shlomo Hamelech* (King Solomon). As I looked around at the wide diversity of the women in attendance, I had to remind myself that we were in an area which most people associate with relaxation. But these women had come to learn and to grow and would share their newfound knowledge with their families and their communities. This was another side of the Catskills I had not anticipated.

Shabbas Nachamu 2000 culminated with the Chazak Concert at Monticello Raceway, sponsored by The Moses and Aaron

Foundation which supports special children through their numerous programs and activities. As we sat in the sold-out bleachers listening to the spirited singing of international entertainer, Avraham Fried, I was once again impressed by the sense of camaraderie Jews of all backgrounds feel when we come together for a shared purpose.

This is what I had found so appealing when I heard the Chasid's friendly announcement that it was time for "Mincha." It reminded me of the old Town Crier who used to swing his lantern down the cobblestone streets of colonial America reassuring everyone within earshot that "all is well." When Jews continue to come together for learning, for doing *chesed* and for afternoon davening it's a reassuring sign that "all is well."

"We Will Have Been Like Dreamers"

It's great that you've come to Israel when everyone is so afraid to travel here right now," said the earnest young man seated across from me in the Atara Café. "But if you really want to do something meaningful, maybe you should consider making *aliyah*." Not an unusual suggestion from an Israeli who's passionate about his country and his religion, except that this blonde-haired, blue-eyed Jew was born a German Christian.

"Are you positive you have no Jewish ancestors?" I ask Nethanel von Boxberg, again. He shakes his head and patiently reassures me, "My family traces their lineage back a thousand years on my mother's side, all the way to Charlemagne." A budding friendship with an Israeli who was living in Germany provided the catalyst for the inquisitive Nethanel to study Judaism. "I jumped into the water and didn't realize how deep it was," he said describing his enthusiastic immersion. The more Nethanel learned about Torah, the more the computer programmer was convinced that it was "the truth."

Several extended visits to Israel culminated with his conversion in 1998 by Rav Avi'or in the Bet Din under the supervision of Rav Chaim Druckman. His parents' reaction? "I have three brothers. One is a marketing executive, one is a doctor, and one is an artist. I am a Jew," he says simply. "Living in Eretz Israel is a *mitzvah* and I'm proud I can fulfill it."

Nethanel was my nephew Eric's roommate during the year he spent in Israel. Now he has a new roommate. Listening intently to this lively exchange between myself, the daughter of Holocaust survivors who was born in Germany and this German ex-patriot is Limor, Nethanel's beautiful new wife of two weeks who is working towards her Master's degree at Hebrew University. Limor informs me that her family was originally from Yemen, but in 1948 they were among the over 800,000 Jews who were rescued from hostile Arab lands and airlifted en masse to Israel during Operation Magic Carpet.

Mission Possible

An evening out in Jerusalem with Limor and Nethanel was not part of the official itinerary of **AFSI** (Americans For a Safe Israel). In November 2002 my husband and I traveled with the group, led by Helen Freedman and Rabbi Bruce Rudolph, on a solidarity mission that included Judea, Samaria, the Golan and Gaza, not your typical tourist destinations. We were a diverse group of thirty-five who resided in states from Oregon to New York, consisting of both couples and singles, observant as well as secular.

There were several **AFSI** repeaters, including Virginia from Texas, a Christian who has visited Israel more than twenty times.

I became aware of the depth of the Christian support for Israel when I spoke with Carrie Burns, Director of the Great News Radio station, who had come with a group of forty-seven from Champaign, Illinois. Each member of the group, which called itself **"Cargo of Care,"** had been sponsored by thirty other people who raised the funds for them to distribute 1,000 teddy bears to children in hospitals all over Israel.

"We wanted to demonstrate our love," Carrie told me. In spite of the anti-Israel newscasts "no one cancelled. Everyone was determined to make the journey."

AFSI's first stop immediately after landing was a welcoming breakfast at the Park Hotel in Netanya, site of the infamous Passover Massacre. As we listened to Eric Cohen, manager and son of the owner, describe the horrific events, workmen were busily renovating the damaged wing of the hotel. This scene was to be repeated throughout our weeklong tour as we observed that the Israeli response to death and destruction was rebirth and renewal.

A Settlement Called Israel

Word had spread like wildfire that a busload of Americans were not only traveling through the West Bank but that we were staying at the Eshel Hashomron Hotel in Ariel, the scene of a terrorist bombing attack just the day before. One of the largest towns in Yesha (Judea, Samaria and Gaza), Ariel is located less than 20 miles east of Tel Aviv. Although it has a population of 20,000 and is home to one of the largest and most impressive colleges in Israel, which we toured, Ariel is still considered a "settlement" by misguided politicians who would like to see it "dismantled" in the name of peace.

When the news reached us that one of the three soldiers who died in the Ariel attack was going to be buried in his hometown of Itamar, we altered our route to attend his funeral. Era Rappaport, olive grower, vintner and our guide par excellence, recited the Tefilla Haderech, (wayfarer's prayer) which took on special meaning as we traveled the roads of Israel.

A prayer for fallen Israeli soldiers was always included in the *Yizkor* service at my Brooklyn *shul*. Now I stood and recited the prayer along with the friends, fellow soldiers and grieving family members of twenty-two year-old Lt. Matan Zagron. The words *". . .may He make peace upon us and upon all Israel"* (Psalm 126) never resonated with more power than here on a hilltop in Samaria.

"This is our strength. They will never defeat us," Matan's sister said with determination in her voice as she looked out over the thousands who had gathered to mourn her brother. The devotion of the women of Israel, the mothers and daughters and sisters we encountered during our trip strengthened each one of us and we resolved to bring their message back to our family and friends in America.

We met unforgettable women like Chana Goffer, who gave an impassioned talk on the grounds of Gilad Farm, an outpost established as a memorial to Gilad Zar, a terror victim. Chana described the reprehensible actions of Defense Minister Binjamin Ben Eliezer who sent 2,000 security troops on Shabbat to dismantle the farm that was built on private land legally owned by the victim's father, Moshe Zar. Several days later we heard the good news that

Ben Eliezer's attempt to use this strategic location as a political scapegoat backfired. He was out of the Labor government and the Zar family was once again in control of their land.

Another heroine, Tahel Ellinson, a pioneer with her husband and young children in the Shimon Hatzadick community, welcomed us to her modest home which provides a crucial Jewish presence in East Jerusalem. Educator Rachel Saperstein left her home of thirty years in Jerusalem and came with her husband, Moshe, to Gaza to teach at Neve Dekalim, a girl's *ulpan*. Also in Gaza, we were left speechless by the quiet strength of Noga Cohen, who lives with her family in Kfar Darom. Mrs. Cohen's three little children lost limbs in one of the first homicide bus bombings. "Our children want to stay here. This is their home," she said gently.

And our own Helen Freedman, whose vision, along with founder Herb Zweibon, has propelled **AFSI** into a powerful advocate for Israel. During our trip we were privileged to have private discussions with Ron Nachman, Mayor of Ariel; MK Michoel Kleiner; Rav Benny Alon, and Moshe Feiglin of Zo Artzeinu and the Jewish Leadership faction.

We relied on photos and videos to help us retain the extraordinary experiences and exceptional people we encountered during our frenetic seven days: watching toys being manufactured in the "occupied territory;" volunteering to pack food for needy families with Yad Eliezer; touring the rooftops of the Old City with Daniel Luria of Ateret Cohanim; reciting *Tehillim* after our attempt to ascend the Temple Mount was stopped by armed guards; watching the construction of new Jewish homes in East Jerusalem with Chaim Silberstein of Beit Orot; the distressing sight of *Kever Rochel* hidden behind cement barricades.

Shabbos Chaya Sarah

I was named for my father's mother who was murdered by the Nazis. Her name was Chaya Sarah, so for me personally the highlight of our trip was *Shabbos Chaya Sarah* (Genesis 23:1) in Hebron. But there are no photos to capture the moment. No videos to record the emotions. Only words to describe the indescribable.

As night falls endless waves of men, women and children

descend from the heights of Kiryat Arba. Thousands of us, Asians and Africans, Europeans and Americans, united by a common ancestor who has guided our footsteps over continents and across oceans, advance towards our sacred destination. Slowly we maneuver the steep, rocky paths of Hebron as soldiers hover over us, *malachim* in green with reassuring guns flapping behind their backs. Finally the multitude converges on the steps of the *Marat Hamachpela* and we soar over the threshold into the realm of our holy *tzadikim*.

I am standing in the towering Yitzhak Hall, but the imposing chamber is dwarfed by the joyful worshippers who crowd into the enormous space. I marvel at the euphoric faces of two young women of Ethiopian descent, whose sweet voices harmonize with the "Lecha Dodi" melodies that reverberate off the surrounding walls, as we turn and bow in unison to welcome the Sabbath Queen. The ingathering of the exiles has begun

Jay Ipson:
The Southern Gentleman
With the Yiddishe Neshama

Richmond was not on our itinerary. The only reason we decided to stop there was to break up the long drive back to Brooklyn from touring the Biltmore Estate in Ashville, North Carolina. It was the kind of spur-of-the moment decision that would ultimately have a powerful effect on the lives of two families.

Quickly scanning the AAA guidebook, I discovered that Virginia had a Holocaust Museum. But it was the description of the special exhibit on a family called "Ipp" that aroused my interest. Ipp was an unusual name. I had heard it only once before.

June 3, 1997
Dear Helen:
   I have just returned from a trip to St. Ottilien where I was given your name by the monks at the monastery. I was on a voyage of discovery with my brother, having been born in St. Ottilien in 1946. I understand that you were also born there.
                              Sincerely, Moshe Ipp

I was born in a hospital located on the grounds of this Benedictine Monastery in Munich, Germany, while my parents, formerly from Poland, were waiting to immigrate to America. In the spring of 1997, I returned to St. Ottilien on my own voyage of discovery and was surprised to find a place of exceptional beauty and serenity. Dr. Moshe Ipp, a pediatrician from Toronto, Canada visited the monastery two months later. He was born there while his parents, Tania and Chaim Ipp, both physicians from Kovno, were caring for survivors like themselves.

Moshe Ipp was the first person I met who had any connection to St. Ottilien. That was about to change. In January of 2000 I attended the landmark Displaced Persons Conference in Washington, DC, where I listened to Professor Robert Hilliard discuss the roles he and Edward Herman, another former G.I., had played in alleviating the suffering of the Jews of St. Ottilien.

The heroic efforts of these extraordinary young men are documented in his revealing memoir, *Surviving The Americans: The Continued Struggle of the Jews After Liberation.* As a result of this encounter, several months later I attended an emotional reunion of St. Ottilien alums in Florida, where I was privileged to meet the other half of the team, Edward Herman, who has since become a good friend.

Robert Hilliard's book was ultimately made into the documentary, *Displaced: Miracle at St. Ottilien,* written, directed and produced by Dr. John Michalczyk, a former Jesuit priest, who is Chair of the Fine Arts Department and Film Studies Program at Boston College. The film has been shown all over the world and had its New York premiere in 2004 at the Museum of Jewish Heritage, where our mothers, Dora Zegerman and Tania Ipp, relived their St. Ottilien experiences once again.

When I inquired about the Ipp family exhibit at the Virginia Holocaust Museum, I was immediately introduced to the museum's founder and executive director. Although his signature ten gallon hat loudly proclaimed "All-American," as I listened to Jay Ipson I detected an unmistakable Yiddish twang to his south of the Mason-Dixon line drawl.

As he proudly welcomed us to his museum with typical southern hospitality, Jay revealed that when his parents immigrated to America, they changed their name from Ipp to Ipson. The special exhibit was actually the harrowing story of his own family's odyssey from their origins in pre-World War II Eastern Europe to their resettlement in Richmond, Virginia, where they prospered in the automotive parts business.

Jay originally opened a modest museum in back of

Richmond's Temple Beth El with artifacts his family had saved. "I was chairman of the Holocaust committee for Federation and would speak to schoolchildren about my experiences," he said. "When we began to outgrow the space in the temple because it became so popular, I was encouraged to go ahead and create a museum of our own."

He found the ideal site, a building that was being used by the government as a storage facility for surplus property. When he contacted state legislator, Eric Cantor, he agreed that converting it into a Holocaust Museum would make good use of the structure and become an asset to the community.

"I bought the building in June 2001 for $1," he told me. "Now we had a building but no money. Volunteers from diverse segments of the community, who supported the project, provided materials and manpower. We removed the debris and scrubbed the entire warehouse. The community provided paint and an architect worked pro bono, donating his time on Sundays."

Jay was six years old when he was imprisoned with his mother, Eta, and father, Izzy, in the Kovno ghetto. Miraculously, they managed to escape and survive by hiding in a 9'x12' hole in the ground dug between two potato cellars on the farm of a righteous Catholic family. This hiding place that he and thirteen others called home for seven months has been painstakingly recreated. As you crawl through the space you begin to comprehend the deprivation of air, light and freedom that Jay and his family experienced.

Other interactive exhibits lead you into a ghetto, through a concentration camp, and on board the doomed ship *St. Louis.* Jay points out that this hands-on approach, combined with an ongoing lecture and film series is geared not only to educate the public about the Holocaust but to stress the importance of respect and tolerance towards all religions and races.

You sense that you are about to embark on a unique journey even before you enter the building. Parked at the entrance is a Holocaust-era German cattle car that Jay, a man of many resources, found and brought back from Germany. The tour of the museum ends symbolically in the famous choral synagogue of Lithuania.

Jay hired an architect who traveled with him to Kovno where he studied the design of the actual synagogue, which he faithfully recreated to serve as a gathering place for community events and *simchas*. And it is here that he recently participated in the Bar Mitzvah of his own grandson. Prominently displayed in a special case is a Torah that was rescued from Kovno by Jay.

I shared with him the story of how I came to be born in St. Ottilien only to discover that he too had a St. Ottilien connection. After they were liberated, he stayed there briefly with his mother who was recuperating from her ordeal in the cellar. Remarkably, he even attended a Jewish school that was set up on the grounds of the monastery. Jay's father, who had been a prominent attorney in Kovno, was put in charge of all the vehicles for UNWRA, dispatching the ambulances to St. Ottilien.

When I put my new friend Jay Ipson of Virginia in touch with my old friend, Moshe Ipp, of Canada I was not at all surprised to learn that, yes, they were related. But because both their fathers were no longer alive they grew up totally unaware of each other's existence. When the two distant cousins and Moshe's mother, Tania, met for the first time in Toronto, they finally had the opportunity to fill in the gaps in each other's lives.

If the story had ended there it would be enough, but my seemingly chance meeting with Jay Ipson produced another significant encounter. When he learned of the St. Ottilien documentary, Jay was eager to have it shown at the museum. Edward Herman, the former G.I. who appears in the film, made sure he was there.

Standing before a hushed audience in the recreated Kovno synagogue, Edward spoke eloquently about the suffering of the survivors he had witnessed at St. Ottilien. And then he went on to praise what he called "the true heroes," extraordinary people like Jay Ipson and his family who had triumphed over their enemies by leading lives filled with purpose and meaning, ultimately enriching their communities and their country.

Not Only To Cure But To Care

Avid armchair archeologists, my husband and I traveled to Israel in March 2005 on a journey of discovery. But it wasn't ancient ruins we looked forward to exploring, but the ancient teachings of one of the greatest men who ever lived. To the Arabs he was Abu Imram Musa ibn Maimun al Qurtubi. The Christians knew him as Maimonides. But to his own people Moses ben Maimon is simply the Rambam.

The occasion of his yahrzeit found us in Tiberius for **The First International Maimonides Conference on Medicine and Ethics Commemorating 800 Years Since the Passing of Maimonides.** The setting was spectacular, springtime on the shores of the Sea of Galilee and the location of Maimonides burial site. The reason why Tiberius became his resting place remains a mystery as does much about the life of this world famous physician, who also mastered the fields of theology, mathematics, law, philosophy, astronomy and ethics.

Here is what we do know. He was born *erev Pesach* 1135 in Cordoba, the capital of Muslim Spain. His mother died in childbirth and he was raised and educated in Hebrew and Jewish studies by his father, Maimon, a renowned judge in the town's rabbinical court. But centuries before Ferdinand and Isabella unleashed the Inquisition, Jews were suffering under the persecution of the fanatical Muslim Almohades. To escape forced conversion to Islam, the family fled to Fez, Morocco where it is believed Maimonides began to educate himself by studying the works of the great physicians Galen and Hippocrates.

Moving briefly to Jerusalem, they were forced to leave because of the Crusader wars raging between Saladin the Great and Richard the Lionhearted. In 1165 the family finally settled in Fostat (old Cairo) where Maimonides became the official leader of Egyptian Jewry and rose to prominence as court physician to the Sultan of Egypt.

Remarkably, Maimonides wrote the commentaries on the **Mishnah** while he was only 23 years old, followed by the **Sefer ha-Mitzvot**, the systematic enumeration of the 613 commandments. He completed his magnum opus, the **Mishnah Torah,** by age 35.

How can an ordinary person even begin to fathom the depth of knowledge and spirituality of one of the greatest Jewish sages in history? To guide us in this daunting task the conference had assembled a team of luminaries from the medical and torah communities around the globe. One of the most revealing presentations was made by Rabbi Dr. Moshe Tendler, Chair of Medical Ethics at Yeshiva University in New York, and a giant in the field of Bioethics who delivered the keynote address, *Health and Healthful Living.*

Dr. Tendler spoke eloquently about the Rambam's connection to a landmark case involving Siamese (conjoined) twins. The year was 1977 and no twins had ever been successfully separated. Dr. C. Everett Koop, the father of pediatric surgery and head of Children's Hospital in Philadelphia, was entrusted with performing the complex surgery. However, since the babies shared a six-chamber heart, only one infant had a chance to survive.

When colleagues questioned Dr. Koop as to why he was delaying the surgery, Dr. Tendler said that the world-renowned physician replied, "Do you know what to do? I don't know what to do. There's a little Jew on the lower east side of New York. When he tells me, then I will know what to do." The little Jew he referred to was none other than Rabbi Moshe Feinstein, a diminutive figure who was the leading *Halachic* authority of his generation. The parents of the conjoined twins were religious Jews who had left the ultimate decision up to this Torah giant whose rulings were accepted worldwide. Rabbi Tendler, Rabbi Feinstien's son-in-law, served as the intermediary between the medical community and the rabbi.

Rabbi Feinstein ruled that since baby A was living off of baby B (whose heart had more chambers), then baby A must be sacrificed to save baby B. He based his ruling on the Rambam's teaching that if a mother's life is in danger, the fetus which is living off the mother must be sacrificed to save the mother. The babies had been born on Rosh Hashanah. The surgery took place on the day after Simchas Torah and it was the first successful separation of conjoined twins in history.

During three days of intense lectures we learned of Maimonides, the nephrologist, who was the first to indicate that the urine can offer clues to illness in the body; the herbalist, who identified the health benefits of garlic, pomegranate, chamomile and oleander; the holistic thinker, who advocated a balanced approach to healing the body and soul; the psychologist, who encouraged regular worship of God to acquire mental health.

Dr. Benjamin Gesundheit, a Pediatric hematologist and oncologist at Soroka University Medical Center, Beer Sheva dedicated his lecture on Maimonides to the memory of Dr. David Appelbaum, who was murdered with his daughter, Nava, in a terrorist attack in Jerusalem on September 9, 2003. According to Dr. Gesundheit, Maimonides cautioned against making Jewish studies your sole profession. Torah, Maimonides taught, is the source but not the end and you must make your impact through other work.

For Maimonides that "other" work was attending to the body and the mind. Dr. Fred Rosner, Professor of Medicine at Mount Sinai School of Medicine and a preeminent authority on Rambam, who has translated his great works from Hebrew into English, made it clear that the Rambam's "attitude toward the practice of medicine came from his deep religious background which makes healing a divine commandment." According to Dr. Rosner, Maimonides was "a physician to sultans and princes and he was a prince to physicians."

Crowns and scepters of a different type were visible in local shops as preparations for the upcoming Purim holiday created a festive mood along the bustling streets of Tiberius. Each time I visit Israel I'm amazed at how these upbeat scenes of everyday life contrast sharply with the images of doom and gloom presented by the mainstream media. The streets teemed with tall, lithe Ethiopian boys, their white kippot enveloping their heads like halos, who mingled easily with Sephardim and Ashkenazim shopping for colorful costumes and *mishloach manot*.

The unique diversity of Israeli society was mirrored by the conference lecturers and attendees including: Dr. Leon Bernstien-Hahn, a urologist from Buenos Aires Argentina; Dr. Kenneth Collins, a family practitioner in Glasgow, Scotland; Nelly Livni, a pathologist from Fez, Morocco; Jocelyne Tovati, a pharmacologist from Paris; Noa Spector Flock, a specialist in body work and movement from St. Petersburgh, Florida,; Andrea Hahn, a vascular surgeon from Otterndorf, Germany; Ophthalmologist Jerry Kobrin and his wife Nancy, a psychoanalyst from St. Paul, Minnesota; Dr. Peter Borenstien of Goteborg, Sweden whose specialty is Neurology, but, given his town's small Jewish population, he also fulfills the dual role of Rabbi and *Mohel*.

Nicole Chamoy, a full time student at Nishmat Seminary from Milwaukee, Wisconsin came with her father because of her interest in medical ethics. Her dad, Dr. Lewis Chamoy, a hand surgeon who is a follower of the Lubavitcher Rebbe, noted that the Rebbe often quoted the Rambam.

Even those retired from the medical field found much to learn from Maimonides. Dr. Michael Davis, the former Dean of the School of Public Health at Hebrew University, and his wife, Betty, a former medical editor of the Israel Journal of Medicine, were dedicated Zionists who had made *aliyah* from England in 1950. Their children served in the Israeli army and now their grandchildren are members of the IDF.

Another transplanted Englishman, Dr. Moshe Kelman, the former Chief Dental officer of Israel who taught ethics at Bar Ilan University, pointed out that "Rambam is the main source of medical ethics for Jews and non-Jews."

These sentiments were echoed by Dr. Michael Schweitzer,

who has a family practice in Stoney Creek, Ontario. "This conference was an eye opener," he agreed. "Rambam has not only influenced our own culture and religion, but the entire world."

Looking out of our modern hotel at the Byzantine/Roman ruins below we were constantly reminded that Israel is a land where the past is always present. During an impromptu conference tour we turned off the main highway and had the opportunity to explore the site of a newly excavated dig where we were treated to an in depth talk by archeologist Dr. Yizhar Hischfeld of Hebrew University. The remains of a *mikvah* and synagogue have already been identified on this site which is believed to have been the seat of the *Sanhedrin* after their expulsion from Jerusalem.

However, it wasn't with the archeologist's spade, but with the meticulous tools of the scholar that the works of the Rambam have been bequeathed to us after 800 years. The continued relevance of his teachings is apparent from the quote delivered by Dr. Samuel Kottek of Hadassah Medical School, *"A physician's duty is not only to cure but to care."* It's a philosophy that continues to speak to us across the centuries.

We're Not In Brooklyn Anymore

Our first trip West was also our first encounter with a kosher bus tour, a sort of Boro Park meets the National Parks scenario, which turned out to be one of the most rewarding travel adventures my husband and I had ever experienced. Black hats and designer handbags soon gave way to baseball caps and fanny packs as thirty-five strangers, men and women of diverse ages, occupations, and backgrounds quickly shed our city slicker selves and morphed into a group of hardy adventurers. We became equally adept at hiking amongst the geysers and mud pots of Yellowstone or rafting down the Tetons' Snake River where the moose and the bald eagles play.

Our journey began in the glitzy caverns of Las Vegas, where on the night of the Lubavitcher Rebbe's yahrzeit Rabbi Mendel Harlig welcomed us for dinner at Chabad of Southern Nevada. Here in the shadow of those flamboyant monuments to the slots, the *Bellagio* and the *MGM Grand*, Chabad had erected a different type of monument, an oasis in the desert where *yiddishkeit* thrives.

A Tale of Two Tribes

And just as the ancient Israelites were accompanied by a Torah on their journey East, the members of our modern-day tribe also carried a Torah on our own trek to Zion, only this one was located in the West. Safely ensconced in specially designed luggage, the scroll was our constant companion for the ten days we explored the natural and man-made wonders of Nevada, Arizona, Utah and

Wyoming. And instead of being sustained by manna from heaven, our meals arrived via the U-Haul van which preceded our motor coach all along our western route.

The long drive to our first destination, Mt. Zion National Park, gave us the opportunity to play Jewish geography, posing an endless stream of questions to satisfy our thirst for connections. We discovered that most of us were either survivors, married to, or children of survivors, displaced persons who had *"all come to look for America."* But whether we identified ourselves as Litvaks or Galicianer, Czechs or Yeckis, we quickly became "touring friends."

Founded by educator Leah Krasnow and Leah Shenker, who have been leading trips throughout America for seventeen years, **Touring Friends'** carefully planned itinerary enabled us to tackle a daunting schedule, five national parks across four states. As we criss-crossed the West in the comfort of our motor coach our veteran tour guide, Enid Bailey, shared valuable information about each region's history, geology and vegetation. And so we added words like sagebrush and paintbrush to our vocabulary and became skilled at identifying these plants that thrive in the western landscape.

You Say Buffalo, I Say Bison

Bison is the technical name for this endangered animal, so at our first sighting we rushed off the bus to capture the Kodak moment. While he seemed more interested in grazing than in us, we had been warned that when this powerful creature decides to move, he moves fast and so when he suddenly stood up we stampeded for the safety of our bus. Turns out he was only stretching.

We were constantly leaving the confines of the bus and interacting with the environment: sailing the pristine waters of Lake Powell as we navigated between the towering red walls of Glen Canyon, touring the inner workings of its colossal dam which ensures that the lights even as far away as Hollywood continue to shine. We were intrigued to learn that the sleepy little town of Kanab, our base on this leg of our journey, was once called Utah's

Little Hollywood where many popular westerns were filmed, including a childhood favorite, "Gunsmoke."

When we finally stood facing the Grand Canyon, I stared at the "Angel's Window" and marveled at how years of wind and rain had conspired to cut a peephole into the massive limestone that soared 9,000 feet above the floor. Here atop the northern rim, this natural picture window in the sky offered us a bird's eye view of the 250 miles of vast deserts and forests that seemed to stretch to eternity. This massive crevice in the earth left us feeling dwarfed while the hoodoos of Bryce Canyon left us speechless. Neither words nor photographs could capture the impact of these fantastic pink and white limestone rock formations that rose thousands of feet and resembled marching giants.

If it's Shabbos, This Must Be Salt Lake City

Salt Lake City, we discovered, was home to a different type of giant, Rabbi Benny Zippel. For the past ten years he and his family have been involved in outreach activities for the entire state of Utah, providing the community with a powerful Jewish presence. Sitting in the impressive new Chabad House and listening to his compelling stories about the challenges of Jewish life in this very Mormon enclave turned out to be a major highlight of our Salt Lake City stopover.

While an interstate Bridge Tournament was in full swing in the room next door, **Touring Friends** welcomed Shabbos in our own private hotel conference room. Our meal was further enhanced by the inspiring anecdotes of fellow traveler, Irwin Benjamin. During his forty years as the owner of a court reporting firm, he came into contact with the famous, Jacob Javits, and the infamous, Son of Sam. Many of the stories he shared came from his entertaining book, *My Secret – Stories of Faith, Family and Reflection.*

For Jews, the ultimate wayfarers, travel can never be just about schlepping up mountains. Rabbi Shabtai Rubel helped put it all in perspective for us during his talk on *Parsha Balak* (Numbers 22:2), which he pointed out alluded to Jewish travel. All of these magnificent sites that we have been privileged to experience, he suggested, not only enable us to further appreciate the awesome power of Hashem, but also give us the opportunity to fulfill our mission as Jews.

And so when we came upon a ponderosa pine tree, which emitted a sweet butterscotch scent a member of the tour suggested we say a *bracha*. When we stopped to enjoy a picnic dinner in a park in Nephi, Utah the men searched the sky, turned eastward and *davened Mincha*. And when the director of our hotel in Jackson Hole, Wyoming rushed onto our bus and told us she couldn't let us depart for the airport without telling us that the entire hotel staff agreed that they had never had such a wonderful group of guests, we all agreed this was a truly a *Kiddush Hashem*.

Glossary

Agunah
A woman unable to obtain official bill of divorce (Get) in accordance with Jewish law.

Aliyah
Rising in location or in personal qualities, as in going to live in Israel.

Avinu
Our father.

Baalei Teshuvah
Those who have returned to their roots and religious observance.

Bamidbar
Desert.

Bashert
Destined, fated, meant to be

Beit Hamidrash
House of study.

Bima
The raised platform or "high place" in the synagogue from which the Torah is read to signify our respect for its holiness.

Bocher
Young man, usually a student, who is a bachelor.

Brachas
Blessings.

Chas v'shalom
G-d forbid, usually said before a negative event you would not want to happen.

Chassid
A member of a Jewish mystic movement founded in the middle of the 18th century by the Baal Shem Tov, a Kabbalist who maintained that G-d's presence was in all of one's surround-

ings and that one should serve G-d in word and deed.
Chassidic groups include the Satmar, Ger, Bobov, Belz and the
Lubavitchers.

Chazak
Be strong.

Chazzunus
Songful prayers.

Chesed
An act of kindness.

Chizuk
Strength and encouragement.

Cholent
Traditional hot stew prepared for eating on the Sabbath.

Chumash
Hebrew Bible.

Davening
Praying.

Derushah
Interpretation of biblical verses.

Emunah
Faith.

Farblongit
Confused and lost.

Farbrengen
Yiddish for "spending time together;" a fabrengen is a gathering of Chassidim when the Rebbe shares his Torah thoughts
and his messages for the Jewish world at large.

Frum
Religiously observant.

Gan Eden
Garden of Eden.

Ger
Convert

Get
Bill of divorce prepared and issued by a rabbinical court.

Glatt Hechsher
Certified markings on products, by an authorized rabbi, identifying the item as kosher and fit for consumption.

Hagar
Mother of Ishmael, who was the son of the patriarch Abraham.

Halacha
Body of Jewish religious law.

Hamantashen
Jam-filled pastry, traditionally baked for Purim, which alludes to the hidden miracles of the holiday.

Hashem
Literally, "The Name." Hashem is the translation of the tetragrammaton, the sacred Hebrew four letter name of G-d.

Hashevaynu
Return us to you.

Hashgacha Protis
Divine Providence.

Heimishe
Homelike, friendly, folksy.

Hineni
Here I am.

Kaddish
Prayer recited by mourners; associated with ascent of the departed soul.

Kesubah
Jewish marriage contract.

Kever Rochel
Tomb of the Matriarch Rachel.

Kiruv
Outreach.

Kiddush Hashem
Sanctification of G-d's name, which occurs when a Jew inter-acts with family, friends and the community in the manner and spirit of the Torah.

Kiruv
Outreach.

Kotel
Wailing or Western Wall in Jerusalem.

Kvell
Glow with pride and pleasure.

L'Chaim.
"To Life!" Traditional Jewish toast.

Lidderlach
Songs.

Malachim
Angels.

Mamish
Really and truly, usually said for emphasis.

Manna
Food miraculously produced by G-d during the Israelites 40 years in the desert.

Marat Hamachpela
Tomb of the Patriarchs in Hebron.

Maven
Expert.

Mechitza
A physical divder used to separate men and women worship-pers so that each will not be distracted from their prayers.

Megillah
The scroll of Esther, read on the holiday of Purim, which relates the miraculous story of how the Jews of Persia were saved from extermination.

Mensch
An upright man, a gentleman, a decent human being.

Mezuzah
A small scoll of parchment, affixed outside to the right side of the doorpost of one's house and the rooms within one's house, on which are written two Biblical passages: "Hear O Israel, the Lord our G-d, the Lord is One. . ." (Deuteronomy 6:4-9) and "And it shall be that if you carefully observe My Commandments. . ." (Deuteronomy 11:13-21).

Midrash
Commentary.

Mikvah
A specially constructed pool of water used for total immersion for the purpose of attaining ritual purity within Judaism.

Mincha
Afternoon prayers.

Mishloach Manot
"Distribution of food portions" during Purim, to increase friendship and unity between Jews.

Mishpacha
Family.

Mitzvah
A commandment.

Modeh Ani
Prayers said upon arising in the morning: "I gratefully thank you, O living and eternal King, for You have returned my soul within me with compassion – abundant is Your faithfulness."

Mohel
One who performs the Brit Milah, the Convenant of Circumcision that G-d established with Abraham and his descendents.

Moshiach
The Messiah, the Anointed One, the Redeemer of Israel.

Nachas
Pride, especially in the achievements of one's children.

Neshama
Soul or spirit.

Niggun
Wordless song.

Parnassa
Livelihood.

Parsha
The weekly Torah reading.

Parve
Containing neither meat nor dairy products.

Pesach
Passover.

Pintele Yid
Essence of Jewishness.

Pushka
Charity box

Rebbetzin
Title used for the wife of a rabbi.

Rosh Chodesh Elul
The first day of the Hebrew month of Elul

Sandak
The person who has the honor of holding the infant during the Brit Milah, ritual circumcision while the blessings are recited.

Sanhedrin
Supreme Court and legislative body of ancient Israel.

Schlep
To drag or haul or to make a tedious journey.

Sabbos Nachamu
Sabbath of Consolation and rejoicing, which immediately follows Tisha B'Av, the saddest day of the Hebrew calendar, when Jews fast to commemorate the destruction of the Holy Temple in Jerusalem.

Shema
"Hear O Israel, the Lord is our G-d, the Lord is One" – the first prayer that a Jewish child is taught to say and the last words a Jew says prior to death. Shema is contained in the mezuzah affixed to the doorpost of the the home, and in the tefillin that a man binds to his arm and head.

Sheitel
Wig traditionally worn by observant women.

Shidduchim
Marriage matches.

Shmattes
Rags.

Shochet
He performs the rital slaughter of mammals and birds in accordance to Jewish dietery laws.

Shomer Shabbos
Sabbath observant

Shtetel
Small town or village in pre-World War II Europe.

Shtreimel
Fur hat worn by certain married Orthodox men.

Shul
Synagogue.

Simcha
Joyous event or celebration.

Tallis Bag
Prayer shawl pouch.

Tanis Esther
Fast observed on the thirteenth day of the Hebrew month of Adar to commemorate Queen Esther's fast at the time of the miracle of Purim.

Tefillin
Ritual object, consisting of black leather boxes containing the four Biblical passages that command the observance of this Commandment and worn by the male on the arm and head during prayer.

Tehillim
Psalms.

Tisha B'Av
Ninth day of month of Av, commemorating the destruction of the Temple in Jerusalem.

Torah
Written law consisting of the five books of Moses: Genesis, Exodus, Leviticus, Numbers, Deuteronomy.

Torat Chaim
Living Torah.

Toyvel
Immersion of food dishes, vessels and utensils in a mikvah to ritually purify them before using.

Tsitsit
Fringed, four-cornered garments worn by males as reminder to observe the commandments, but not required of females since it is classified as a time-related commandment.

Tsuris
Troubles.

Tyre Kinderlach
Dear little children.

Tzadikim
The pious, righteous patriarchs: Abraham, Isaac and Jacob.

Tzedakah
Charity, specifically helping someone less fortunate than oneself. From the root "Tzedek," meaning "Justice" or "Righteousness."

Tznius
Modesty

Ulpan
School in Israel designed to help new citizens integrate into the social, cultural and economic life of the country by learning the basic language skills of conversation and writing.

Upsheren
Hair-cutting ceremony performed when the male child is three years old.

Vaad Hatzola
Orthodox rescue organization.

Yahrzeit
Date on which the death of a loved one is commemorated.

Yiddin
Jews.

Yiddish Neshama
Jewish soul.

Yiddishkeit
A feeling of identification with and emotional attachment to the Jewish people.

Yizkor
Memorial service when a Jew pays homage to his forebearers, based on the firm belief that the living, by acts or piety and goodness, can redeem and bring honor to the deceased.

Zayde
Grandfather.